Praise for
Once I Was You—Adapted for Young Readers

"I can't stress enough how important it is to read stories like Maria Hinojosa's. All the historical horrors of the American immigrant system. All the loving amid the horror. All the imagining of a new world where we all belong."
—Ibram X. Kendi, National Book Award–winning author of *Stamped from the Beginning* and *How to Be an Antiracist*

"Practically a how-to manual on ways to stand up, be counted, and be heard. Moreover, Hinojosa describes how she came to use her voice to help others. Wepa!"
—Actress and author Sonia Manzano, "Maria" on *Sesame Street*

"Electric. Engaging. *Once I Was You* for young readers is the perfect introduction to complex topics like immigration and racism in the United States. This book is brimming with hope and joy, and readers of all ages will be uplifted by Maria Hinojosa's life experiences, power, and incredible storytelling magic."
—Gabby Rivera, author of *Juliet Takes a Breath*

"In a voice that is at turns thoughtful and hilarious, Hinojosa takes readers on a ride of not only her own journey toward amplifying her voice but also the journey of an entire family and community demanding to be heard. Full of equal parts feeling and fact, *Once I Was You* will inspire young readers for generations to come."
—Elizabeth Acevedo, author of *The Poet X*

"This is a story of a young woman whose voice has become indispensable in understanding the American experience. And yes, her voice has produced a change in all of us who have stopped to listen to what she has to say."
—Benjamin Alire Sáenz, #1 *New York Times* bestselling author of *Aristotle and Dante Discover the Secrets of the Universe*

"Maria Hinojosa is hands down one of the most important, respected, and beloved cultural leaders in the Latinx community. . . . Hers is a voice we need to hear at this moment in our country!"
—Julia Alvarez, author of *How the García Girls Lost Their Accents*

ONCE
I WAS YOU

ADAPTED FOR YOUNG READERS

MARIA HINOJOSA

Simon & Schuster Books for Young Readers
NEW YORK • LONDON • TORONTO • SYDNEY • NEW DELHI

SIMON & SCHUSTER BOOKS FOR YOUNG READERS
An imprint of Simon & Schuster Children's Publishing Division
1230 Avenue of the Americas, New York, New York 10020
This work is a memoir. It reflects the author's present recollections of
her experiences over a period of years.
© 2020 by The Hinojosa Corporation
Young readers edition © 2022 by Simon & Schuster, Inc.
This young readers edition is adapted from *Once I Was You* by Maria Hinojosa,
published by Atria Books in 2020.
Jacket illustration © 2022 by Paola Escobar
Jacket design by Laura Eckes © 2022 by Simon & Schuster, Inc.
All rights reserved, including the right of reproduction in whole or in part in any form.
SIMON & SCHUSTER BOOKS FOR YOUNG READERS
and related marks are trademarks of Simon & Schuster, Inc.
For information about special discounts for bulk purchases, please contact Simon &
Schuster Special Sales at 1-866-506-1949 or business@simonandschuster.com.
The Simon & Schuster Speakers Bureau can bring authors to your live event.
For more information or to book an event, contact the Simon & Schuster Speakers
Bureau at 1-866-248-3049 or visit our website at www.simonspeakers.com.
Interior design by Hilary Zarycky
The text for this book was set in Adobe Garamond.
Manufactured in the United States of America
0722 FFG
First Edition
2 4 6 8 10 9 7 5 3 1
CIP data for this book is available from the Library of Congress.
ISBN 9781665902809
ISBN 9781665902823 (ebook)

Para mi hija, my one and only daughter, Yurema.
Tú y solamente tú eres mi sol con esa sonrisa de amor.

For all the girls and boys who, like me, weren't born in this country and aren't going anywhere.

And for my mom, Berta y Bertha. Con amor.

Contents

Introduction

In February 2019, I met a beautiful girl from Guatemala at the airport in McAllen, Texas, which sits near the US-Mexico border. Immigration agents had taken her from her uncle and kept her in a caged-in detention center. Now she was being taken someplace else on a plane. She was terrified and being transported by strangers. But she and I connected, if only for a moment.

She was in shock and looked numb as she waited in the airport along with about ten other kids between the ages of five and fifteen. All of them were silent, dejected, withdrawn, and just plain sad. That's what most stood out to me about these kids: how sad they all looked.

I smiled and asked her how she was doing. But then one of the handlers, or in my view traffickers, told me I couldn't talk to her. Maybe the girl will remember me because I stood up to the man who was the boss of the group. I told him I was a journalist and that I had a right to speak to the kids. He said no and I answered him back. I spoke up loudly in the middle of the airport and told this man that these children were loved and wanted in this country and that they deserved to have a voice.

That girl is one of the reasons I decided to write this book.

I was not born in this country, but I had the privilege to become a citizen of the United States by choice later in life, when I was about thirty years old. While I love this country because it is home, I also made the decision to become a citizen out of fear that one day immigration officials would turn me away at the border or at an airport when I presented my green card. It's strange to use the words "love" and "fear" when you are talking about a country, but I feel both emotions toward my adopted homeland. It is the place where I fully embraced my identity as a Latina and where I learned to ask hard questions as a journalist. The reason I'm still here is because I want to help make this country better, and one way I can do that is through my journalism.

Journalists are the people who keep us informed about what's going on in the country and the world. I learned this lesson as a little girl watching the news on TV.

Imagine having a TV the size of a washing machine in the middle of your living room. I know people have BIG TVs now but they are flat. No, the TV sets that I am talking about from the 1960s were huge, clunky wooden boxes with built-in speakers and big knobs. The pictures they showed only appeared in black and white.

My family was lucky enough to buy a used one. Watching

the news on that television set was my first interaction with American journalism. The anchors who delivered the news were always white men in suits, white men who spoke English without any accent, without a single hair out of place, and who appeared not to have any feelings. These were the people given the power to tell us what was happening and what mattered in the world.

I watched the news on television every night. By the time I was nine years old, we had bought a color TV that sat in our kitchen where we could watch it from the dinner table. Our familia in Mexico was horrified that we had become those people—gringos who had a TV in the same place where they ate! But the world was too dramatic not to want to watch. There was a war going on in Vietnam. Protests across US cities. Refugees fighting to survive in their new home. Love and hate playing out in the streets.

But my family, who came from Mexico, were immigrants to this country, newcomers and dreamers, because of my father's job as a scientist. Our stories, and people who looked like us, were nowhere to be seen on the news or in mainstream media. This made me feel invisible.

I looked for myself everywhere in the media. In *Time* magazine. On *60 Minutes*. In the *Chicago Sun-Times*. Nada.

I searched through store racks that sold products personalized with names on them. I looked for stickers, buttons, notebooks . . . anything to affirm in the written word that I existed. The displays seemed to carry every name you could possibly imagine, except for one. Mine. Maria.

That feeling of invisibility followed me everywhere I went in this country, the United States of America. The places where I did see and hear people who looked and sounded like me were barrios that looked abandonados—deserted neighborhoods with no trash pickup, no playgrounds, and broken windows. Still, these places were filled with life and color and the language of love.

Buenos días, Señora!

Que lindo día!

Que le vaya bonito!

Que bello, mi amor!

Mi querida, mi sol, mi vida!

I didn't know it then, but I wanted to tell the stories of the people I saw and knew in the barrio. In the beginning, I didn't know how. I did not feel smart enough to be one of those people on the TV news who appear to have no feelings and never have a single hair out of place. I was the opposite of all that. I was a woman and a Latina. And I had a lot of hair.

I became obsessed with understanding the invisibility that I felt and fighting against it. The lack of Latinos and Latinas in the media marked me. It made me want to do something to change the reality I had been presented with. There are so many important experiences like this that you will have during your life. I hope this book makes you pay attention to the seeds being planted in you that will sprout as you get older.

For me, the seeds of that invisibility sprang forth and inspired me to become a radio and TV journalist and work at NPR, CNN, PBS, and many other media companies. Along the way, people told me I was too close to the stories I wanted to tell to be objective. *You are too Mexican-y. Too immigrant-y. Too feminist-y. Too left-y. Too ungrateful* and maybe even *too unpatriotic.* After working for all those companies and proving myself over and over again, I finally decided to go out on my own.

I took a huge risk and left corporate media to create my own media company, Futuro Media, in 2011. I became the first Latina to found a national independent nonprofit newsroom. I took control of the microphone and the camera. I was no longer just a reporter on the airwaves, but also the executive calling the shots.

One day in 2016, as a journalist with thirty years of experience, I appeared on cable news to talk about immigration. The other guest, who supported the policies of then-President Donald Trump, dared to refer to immigrants, fellow human beings, as "illegals."

In this moment, I was the opposite of invisible. I was on prime-time cable television, being watched in the homes of millions of people. On live TV, I let loose. "There is no such thing as an illegal human being," I said in response to the other guest speaker. "'Illegal' is not a noun! Never use that term to refer to a human being. It was the first thing the Nazis did to the Jews. They labeled them an 'illegal people.'"

In fact, that's how the Holocaust started, but I didn't get a chance to say that. TV sound bites are ninety seconds. I had to wrap it up. But if I'd had more time, I would have shared what Elie Wiesel, a Holocaust survivor and winner of the Nobel

Peace Prize, told me. If you say an entire people are illegal, as opposed to using the term to describe a crime one may have committed as an individual, then you are taking away an entire people's humanity. Laws exist to stop people from doing things that are deemed illegal and bad for society. But a whole group of people cannot be considered illegal just because of their religion or where they were born. Calling a person illegal is like saying they don't have a right to exist, and that's a dangerous idea.

Within hours of my TV appearance, the clip had been shared on social media thousands of times. What helped this moment go viral (apart from the words) was that I was correcting a dude on TV. The way it came out, I looked like I did a double take and then an oh-no-you-didn't shoulder twist (I'm a trained boxer so I can't help myself!) as I scolded him (there was a finger involved).

There is a saying in Mexican Spanish: No hay mal que por bien no venga; there is no bad from which good cannot come. Okay, that is a clunky way of saying that if something bad happens, you can always find the silver lining. The discomfort I felt as a kid planted a seed in me that led me onto this path. Being a journalist is a job, yes, but for me it's also a mission. I have committed my career to scratching that massive itch of invisibility. I have continued to fight against allowing other people to tell our stories, people who did not really understand or know us, and refused to give them the power to control the narrative.

The years of the Trump presidency brought a specific kind

of horror to the Latino and immigrant experience. This man began his campaign for president by riding down a fake gold escalator and then saying that he wanted to build a wall because Mexico was sending "criminals" to come to the United States. (To be clear, that is a lie. There are fewer criminals among immigrants in the US than among people born here.)

Once he was in the White House, when families tried to come to this country for help, the US government started taking children and babies away from their parents. It's because of journalists and whistleblowers who snuck out a phone recording that we were able to hear the voices of these kids crying as they were held in cages and given blankets that are essentially made out of aluminum foil.

Let's be clear: The ugly hatred against immigrants, Latinos and Latinas, Asian people, and indigenous and Black folks did not start with Donald Trump. The anti-immigrant policies we have lived through and still experience today were not started by him. He made everything worse, but the groundwork was there long before he came along.

If we want to atone for our sins and heal these collective wounds, our beloved country has to come to terms with how it was founded. The men and women who first came here from Europe were conquerors and settlers as much as they were also people searching for freedom and a dream. They founded this country on guns and power and used the idea of race to hold onto both. Just like this country was built on anti-Black and anti-Indigenous hatred, it has survived on anti-immigrant and anti-refugee hatred. It's all been on the books, in our laws, written by white men in government.

The country that says it loves immigrants and refugees, and worships one particularly imposing lady called the Statue of Liberty, has undermined its own motto of accepting "the huddled masses" on its shore every century of its existence by encouraging its citizens to hate people whose only real difference is that they were not born on this land.

I don't want anyone to feel invisible in this country because, guess what? We are all a part of it.

This country of ours has used and abused us from the very beginning. It's a hard lesson to learn, but acknowledging the truth is the first step to bringing about change in a positive direction.

We need to learn about what really happened here and the parts of American history that have been left out of the history books—not just the events that make the US look good from the perspective of you-know-who.

The poet Emma Lazarus wrote the poem on the base of the Statue of Liberty: "Give me your tired, your poor, Your huddled masses yearning to breathe free, The wretched refuse of your teeming shore." Those words set the intention of this nation—to love and welcome people from faraway lands into the fold. The US has been that country in the past, welcoming refugees at various times throughout its history from Vietnam, Ethiopia, Cuba, Ukraine, Burma, Argentina, and many other countries, with ordinary Americans showing up and opening their homes to help refugees resettle in places like Texas, Ohio, Nebraska, and Arizona. And it can be that country again in the future only if we all make it that way, together.

This book is about how it all started for me (and about how it's going). I will tell you the story of how I arrived in the US, what it was like to grow up as a little Mexican girl on the South Side of Chicago, and the experiences that motivated me to become a journalist. It was that work that eventually brought me to McAllen, Texas, to cover the immigration situation at the border, where I met that little girl at the airport.

I don't know where she is now, but I hope that one day she will read these words. I've always wanted her to know that I heard her and I saw her and I never forgot her. This country was made for people like her. I hope she makes it here and this country really becomes hers.

I told her I wanted to hear her words. I told her, *I see you because once I was you.*

CHAPTER I

Once Upon a Time in Mexico

I was born in Mexico City during the rainy season in the summer of 1961, when it wasn't yet one of the largest cities in the world the way it is now. Back then, palm trees grew in the middle of downtown and my sister and brothers played hide-and-go-seek in the streets.

On most days you could look out the window from our house and see the snow-capped peaks of the Popocatépetl and Iztaccíhuatl volcanoes. Of course, I didn't notice any of this as a little baby, but later as a kid I would come to know all the things my sister and brothers already knew about Mexico City. I would spell the volcanoes' names out phonetically so that I could learn how to say them—PO-PO-KA-TEP-UH-TL and EE-STAK-SEE-WAH-TL. I grew up hearing and speaking Spanish as my native tongue. But these names aren't actually Spanish. They are Nahuatl, a language spoken by the Nahua people, who are descendants of the Aztecs. The story goes that Popocatépetl and

Iztaccíhuatl were in love. Anywhere else they might just be two volcanoes, but in Mexico they became star-crossed lovers.

The scents and flavors of Mexico were intense and unforgettable. I can never forget the smell of ripe mango in the morning for breakfast, key lime squeezed on top of papaya, the pungent aroma of cilantro and garlic, and Mexican rice seasoned just so with tomato and achiote for that vibrant pinch of red—the secret ingredient that all Mexican moms somehow know to throw in.

Whenever my mom took us to the mercado, it was like sensory overload. In the open-air market underneath a covered roof, each section had different smells. My nose would go crazy as we walked by the corner that sold pork and chicharrón. The man who worked the stall fried pork skin right in front of your face in a huge vat of boiling oil. If you took another hundred steps forward, you would end up in the corner of the market where they sold fresh cut flowers. Now you'd be smelling the roses and lilacs.

Turn another corner and you'd breathe in the scents of oregano and cumin at the stalls that sold spices. The fruit section was more about color than smell. Ruby red strawberries were piled high in perfect pyramids. Mangoes mimicked the colors of a sherbet sunset with shades of pink, orange, and golden yellow. They were ripe and ready to be peeled. Every time I ate one, the mango hairs always got stuck in my teeth. I loved them as much as I hated them.

That very first year in Mexico, though, I was still a baby in my mother's arms. I was stuck to her like chicle, like gum.

Everywhere she went, I went. Meanwhile, my sister, seven-year-old Bertha Elena, followed by my brothers Raúl, five, and Jorge, two, were let loose. Our neighborhood was known as Colonia Narvarte; the colony of Narvarte. Being a kid there meant being free. The kids were always out in the street jumping rope or playing hopscotch. Or they hung out in the parks together, which were massive and green 365 days a year because Mexico City never gets cold like that.

There was familia in abundance. But there was no TV. No iPhones or iPads. No radio really, except for the stations that played Mexican music or radio novelas. There were no plastic toys. No *Sesame Street*. And yet everyone had a great time. My siblings made things up because they had no choice. They acted out entire dramas and invented new games in the parks and palm-lined streets of la Colonia Narvarte. There was nothing to be afraid of. If you fell off a swing, you might come home with a few scrapes, but as long as nobody was crying everything was fine. You were safe and loved and fed. And there was no English to be heard anywhere.

Sometimes my sister and brothers played upstairs in our bedrooms. The same mercado where my mom shopped daily (people barely used refrigerators back then) had a children's section where a few stalls sold papier-mâché miniatures of everything you could buy at the market. They had baby fruits and vegetables painted in bright colors and even tiny wooden kitchen replicas filled with teeny ceramic dishes and bowls—"estilo de una vajilla típica del pueblo"—that my sister and primas would use to make pretend meals.

When I came into the picture, my mom began to rely a lot on my big sister. As the oldest, Bertha Elena was the one in charge and I idolized her my entire childhood. She had long, jet-black hair, thick eyebrows, and a sharp Aztec nose como la bella Iztaccíhuatl. Even though I was Mom's chicle, as I grew older my sister became the role model I looked up to. Everything she did seemed so hip and modern. She was already wearing perfectly coordinated outfits. She showed up to play dates wearing a petticoat, white dress, and white patent leather shoes with bows in her hair, her skin looking even more chocolatey in comparison to her starched white dress.

Bertha Elena played house with us and made sure my brothers didn't destroy everything around them. Sometimes she dressed them in matching clothes because that was the style, everything matching. In fact, Bertha, my mom, and I sometimes wore matching outfits too. (Yes, my sister is named after my mom and my brother Raúl is named after my dad. Show me you're Mexican. . . .)

Raúl was known for being somewhat out of control. He was always falling off things and hitting his head. By six years old, he'd already had one or two concussions. Raúl talked so much that one time my mother hit him on the top of his head with a plastic plate and broke it. That's not something that would be considered acceptable nowadays, but things were a little wack back then when it came to corporal punishment.

My brother Jorge, who'd enjoyed being the baby of the family for two years until I arrived, was now the third child out of four. In many ways, he had a hard time being overshadowed by his louder older brother, but some would call that dirty laundry, so allí muere.

Since she was older and better behaved, my sister went to church with our grandmother several times a week. Catholic masses were always said in Latin back then. Bertha Elena (we called her by her full name) would sit in the church pew, perfectly quiet, not understanding a single word, and watch the other congregants to figure out when to stand and kneel at the right times. This went on for an entire hour. Sometimes she saw our grandmother beating her chest and saying "mea culpa" over and over again. It scared her. The statue of Jesus Christ being crucified was also hard to look at. The wounds on his hands and feet where he was nailed onto the cross looked so real. If you've been to a church in Latina America, you know what I'm talking about. Who needs a gory movie when you can just go to church and see the statues of Jesus dripping blood from his head with the crown of thorns and his life-size feet where the nails were gashed in and all the way through to the wooden crucifix?

Church was always a little weird, but Bertha Elena liked that she got to wear her black leather shoes and a mantilla, a veil made out of lace. Afterwards, she and our grandmother would stop and buy a snack from one of the women outside. The ladies wore long braids and spoke accented Spanish because they were usually Nahua or Zapotec. They sold freshly sliced jicama with chili and lime or freshly toasted chicharrón, thin and crunchy and warm, out of huge straw baskets. That made the entire ordeal worth it.

There is a common saying that it takes a village to raise a child, so I guess we would have said toma un pueblito, but our family was so big it was like we were our own pueblito, and we took care of one another. My dad was usually busy working three different jobs to support us and follow his dream of being a research doctor and finding a way to help the deaf to hear if they wanted to. The only way my mom was able to handle taking care of four kids under the age of seven in her home was with the help of her hermanas, cuñadas, and primas who were around us all the time.

We lived on a street called Eugenia. My mother's eldest sister, Lila, lived a few blocks away on Pythagoras Street. That was another one of those words I had to practice to say right—PEE-TAG-OH-RAS en Español.

Lila had five kids. My mother's other sister, Gloria, had seven. Her brother Hermilo had five and her brother Raphael had four. Altogether, including my siblings and me, that's twenty-five kids, and that was basically what life was about for me and my mom and sister and brothers. When we all got together it was as many kids as one classroom!

Every Monday, Wednesday, and Friday, after school ended at two p.m., the entire extended family would gather at someone's house for the traditional comida del mediodía. This is the main midday meal, kind of like an extended lunch, that starts at three o'clock and is supposed to end at five. Often, though, it goes on until seven or even eight in the evening with something called la sobremesa ("the after table," which includes coffee, dessert, and sometimes tequila), by which time people are ready to have la cena or dinner. There used to be a lot more time off back then. You didn't live to work. You lived. And you worked some—unless you were my hyper-focused father who worked because he loved it and was on a mission.

Whoever was hosting la comida had to pay for all the food, prepare the meal, and take care of serving everybody. Can you imagine being responsible for feeding fifteen, sometimes twenty or even twenty-five people? That's a lot of work. And it usually meant that the women were doing all of it and serving the men. When I think back to the way Mexico was and still is, that is the part I dislike most—how the men are always being served by the women. That is one seed that was planted early in my body and soul that I rejected thoroughly.

The women in my family didn't complain, though. They helped whoever was hosting in the kitchen. That's where they worked and gossiped and joked and gave all the kids hugs. Once the kids had eaten and the rest of the meal was ready, the adults sat down to eat.

Our grandfather showed up to every single comida del mediodía even though he no longer lived with our grand-mother. His skin was the color of smooth dark brown leather. He always wore rimmed glasses and a suit and tie, and held a cigarette in his hand till I forced him to quit when I was a teen-ager. This was the only time my grandfather and grandmother saw each other anymore; it was one of those strange things that happens in Mexican families. They just never told us kids what was going on between them.

Abuelito always sat at the head of the table. My sister

remembers him giving all the kids coins to go to a store known as La Miscellanea or the Miscellaneous Store. Their chore was to buy a Coke and an orange Fanta to bring back to the adults who were eating. It was a way of keeping the kids out of the house so the adults could have a moment of peace. There was always money left over for each of the kids to get a piece of candy. Their favorites at that time were pirulín, a colorful lollipop in the shape of a long cone, Chiclets gum, especially the lavender and pink colors, and Gansitos, which were little cakes covered in chocolate and filled with strawberry jelly.

La comida del mediodía wasn't about the food. It was about being together. Since these meals took place at a regular time and place every week, anyone could just show up.

On Fridays, the meal was always at mi Tío Gordo's house. Gordo means "fat," so his nickname was "my uncle, the fat man," but in Spanish it was meant more as a term of affection than anything else. Mi Tío Gordo was a jokester and would do dramatic things to get a laugh. Sometimes he had one too many tequilas and would end up throwing my family's shoes out his apartment window just for fun. During the sobremesa, made up of chisme and chit-chatting, Tío Gordo would take the crumbs leftover from bolillos, Mexican bread rolls, and roll them up into tiny little balls. Then he'd throw them at my mami and my aunts—mi Tía Gloria, mi Tía Marta, mi Tía Carmelita, and the eldest, mi Tía Licha—aiming to get the little bread balls to fall into their cleavage. The women all covered their chests with their hands and continued talking. Next he tried to get the balls into their glasses of Coke. By the end of sobremesa, all the women had one hand covering their glass and another hand blocking their chest and they carried on entire conversations this way. The kids just laughed.

Sometimes mi Tío Benito was there. He was the uncle who later took me to see my first bull fight in the heart of Mexico City. He was funny, wore thick glasses, had tight curly hair, and, like his glasses, his lips were thick. He specialized in chistes and cuentos, in telling and singing jokes, rhyming jokes, off-color jokes, jokes that involved accents and reenactments, and jokes about our family. He would bring his guitar and make up songs to sing about each family member but actually teasingly and lovingly insult them bajita la mano. Everyone laughed at one another other. Remember, there was no Internet back then. People talked to each other face-to-face and the shade was real. People from Mexico City don't play when it comes to dark, biting, and often belittling humor, so if you could spit it, you had to be able to catch it too.

Sometimes mi Tía Maria Cobadonga (I loved saying her name because it had so many syllables that it was like a haiku poem) would show up and tell stories about how the spirits came to visit her. Everybody knew she was a spiritual medium who had contact with the other side. Even though she was only in her thirties, her hair had gone completely white. Everyone told stories that were dramatic (so Mexican) but her stories were *super* dramatic. She would reenact the way people walked with a particular gait or their particular way of talking. And she would usually have the women running to the bathroom because they peed a little when they laughed and just couldn't hold it any longer. These were the first seeds of storytelling that were planted in me.

My grandmother's sisters who never married, mi Tía Carmelita and mi Tía Licha, often showed up too. Since they were both single, they lived and traveled everywhere together. They both had hair that was tight and curly and their lips and noses were thick and round, different from my mom's and sister's Aztec noses. Their brothers looked the same way, except they were bald. Looking at them, it made sense that somehow people from Africa had made their way to Mexico, to my Mexican family.

In our life in Mexico, my siblings and I saw our entire extended family three times a week. We felt completely supported and loved by lots of people who were also our blood relatives—grandparents and aunts and uncles and cousins. How was it possible that my mom and dad would make the decision to leave all of that behind?

My mom, like my grandmother, is what you call in Mexico una pata de perro or a dog's foot. It means that she likes to be outside in the world, like the stray dogs that roam the streets of Mexico City. My mother learned at a young age from her own mother to go out and explore, however she could. She was never afraid to go anywhere or to speak to anyone.

In 1961, the University of Chicago came calling for my dad. They admired his research and wanted his brain—his mission and passion had earned him a job offer. Dad hated the idea of leaving Mexico. Like most immigrants, he really didn't want to turn his back on his homeland, though he was tired of working three jobs. It was my mom who convinced him to say yes.

The University of Chicago was offering him an opportunity to make his dream a reality. My dad thought he could help do something most people considered impossible: give hearing back to those who wanted it. It hadn't been easy for him to listen to his own family tell him his dream was loco, una locura, una ilusion. But the seed was planted and he never gave up and now he was off!

My mom was a pata de perro and my dad was a dreamer dedicated to looking at teeny tiny particles in the electron microscope ten hours a day. They were both out-of-the-box thinkers. So, almost one year after I was born, they took the leap to leave their country and come to the United States. Neither one of them ever had a seed planted in them that made them want to leave Mexico, but la vida les mando este regalo. Was it a gift or something else?

CHAPTER 2

Coming to America

Soon after my dad accepted the job offer from the University of Chicago, he was granted US citizenship as an immigrant "of extraordinary ability." I mean, I know that is some elitist BS, but I did tell you Papi was a genius. He made the trip north from Mexico City to Chicago by plane a few months later. The plan was for my dad to start his new job, get settled, and find an apartment in Chicago for all of us to live in. My mom and us kids would stay behind in Mexico until he was ready for us to join him.

This is the story of how my mom and me and my siblings came to "America. . . ." But let's correct one common assumption right now. When I was in Mexico, I was already in America. Mexico is part of North America, so I was born in North America. Then there is South America and Central America. So really, *all* of us in the Americas are Americans. Acting as if only people in the US are Americans is one of my pet peeves.

On the day we were set to leave for the US, my mom, a tiny, five-foot-tall woman with black hair, thick arched eyebrows, and full red lips, was dressed to the nines in kitten heels and a velvet skirt. She woke up early to prepare her four young children for their very first plane ride together. We would fly from Mexico City to Dallas, Texas, and then in Dallas transfer to another plane to Chicago, where my dad would meet us. The year was 1962, and yes, there were planes back then, but most people didn't use them. Traveling by plane was reserved for special occasions and for the super rich who could afford it. This was definitely a special occasion, because my family was not super rich.

I was quietly resting in my mother's arms as we made our way through the airport and onto the plane. But my brother Jorge, who was three years old, screamed during the entire plane ride, which apparently was funny and unforgettable. "Un cai, un cai!" he kept yelling out the plane window. He was trying to say, "Nos cayemos, nos cayemos!" or, "We're falling, we're falling!" but he didn't know how to say the word yet.

In between Jorge shouting, my brother Raúl was busy asking my mother a bazillion questions because he was the brainiac of the family and wanted to know everything about what was going on. How high was the plane? Why weren't we falling to the ground? How exactly did la gravedad, gravity, work?

Bertha Elena, the oldest at seven years old, was looking out the window and crying. She was, perhaps, the only one of us who understood what exactly was going on. We were leaving our native country. We had all been born in Mexico, and now we were leaving it behind and moving to a place we had never been to before—a cold city in the middle of the United States called Chicago.

When I was younger, I used to joke and say I had ni voz ni voto; I had neither a voice nor a vote in the decision to leave Mexico and come to the United States. For many years, that was how I understood my arrival in this country. I entered quietly in the security of my mother's arms, wearing a white frilly dress that she had made especially for this trip. My big black eyes were fascinated by everything and yet not a peep came out of my mouth because I was a perfect baby. Mom's chicle. I was just there for the ride.

As I got older, I began to have questions about how I came to the US, so I asked my mom to tell me more about how we got here. It turned out there was a part of the story that had been left out.

We thought the scariest thing that had happened on the trip was my baby brother screaming about the plane falling. In fact, flying in the air was the easy part. Things got a little strange, though, when my mother and us kids made our way to the immigration area at the Dallas airport.

Nowadays when people come into the US from another country, they are required to go through an immigration check where government officers inspect their passports and papers to decide whether they have permission to enter. There are usually two lines: one for US citizens and permanent residents, and one for everyone who holds citizenship in another country. Mexico and the United States sit next to each other geographically and share a border. A lot of the Southwestern United States, including Texas, California, and the Northwest almost up to Canada, used to be a part of Mexico. The two countries have a long history of people going back and forth between them, but unfortunately, they haven't always had a friendly relationship. Even though on the ground people who live en la frontera get along perfectly well with one another and everybody else, there's still this pinche fight brought on by the US, history, and well, racism.

Here is your trigger warning. The story always starts out nice, like my sweet life en la Colonia Narvarte. Happy Mexicans couldn't care less about what's happening in gringolandia because they know the world does not revolve around the United States, but some white supremacists were not going to let things end there. Don't get sucked into the lie of American exceptionalism. "Exceptionalism" is a false belief that this country and only this country is the best at everything. Remember, I told you we're going to break some historical myths. Racism is nasty and hurtful and you're about to see it up close.

In 1916, Tom Lea Sr., the mayor of El Paso, Texas, came up with an ugly notion that Mexicans were not clean. Based on this belief, he and others began calling people like me "dirty Mexicans." The phrase became a racial slur because it used hateful words to insult and damage perceptions of other people. Do you know that saying, "Sticks and stones may break my bones, but words will never hurt me"? Well, it's only half true, because words have power and those specific words ended up being used to create laws to keep people like me, Mexicans, as well as other Black and Brown people who were not born here, out of the United States.

Because of Mayor Lea's words, the US government set up a fumigation facility in El Paso on the US-Mexico border. Mexicans who had been used to crossing the border daily to go to their jobs in Texas were now forced to be inspected for cleanliness before they were allowed into the United States. What started as a process of immigration officers looking at Mexican bodies to see if they had wounds or fever or any kind of sickness quickly turned into ordering Mexicans to take baths in gasoline and spraying their clothing with poisonous Zyklon B gas to disinfect them.

This went on for forty years. Can you imagine having to go through that ordeal every day just so that you can go to work or visit your family?

That brings me back to my mom's story about our arrival in America. After we got off the plane at the Dallas airport, my mom walked us through the airport and got into the immigration line for US citizens and residents.

My mom knew that she had privilege. Even though my family didn't have money, we had been granted green cards because of my dad's job as a highly skilled research doctor who was working on important, life-changing technology at the University of Chicago. Actually, they were more of a faded lime green with squiggly lines through our faces. It was called a resident "alien" card, even though the only thing that made us different from US citizens was the fact that we were not born in this country. And that's what they still called it until 2021, when President Joe Biden officially prohibited the use of the word "alien" from all government documents.

Once we got to the front of the line at the immigration checkpoint and it was our turn, my mom walked with all of us to the first open booth. Behind it stood an immigration agent who was as tall as a redwood tree, a Texan with blond hair and a mustache. My mom felt like a tiny shrub compared to him. Despite wearing an immigration agent's uniform, he looked like a guy from a Hollywood movie, so she imagined he would be nice. My mom approached him with a smile on her face and extended her hand with our five green cards—our resident alien cards that she understood gave us permission to come into the United States.

That's why when the agent began to study our faces very closely, my mom began to get a little exasperated. I started fidgeting in her arms, so she held me more tightly to her chest. My sister Bertha Elena pulled my two brothers closer to her as well. Then the agent's eyes darkened and zeroed in on me like a hungry zopilote, a vulture ready to eat me. My mom recoiled.

"Ma'am, you are welcome to come into the United States," the officer said with a thick Texas drawl, "but this baby girl, she's got a little rash on her and we're going to have to put her into quarantine here. So you and the rest of your kids can go on to Chicago and we'll just keep the baby here." The only reason I had a rash was because I had to use a scratchy blanket on the plane in place of my normal blanket that had been packed away for the move.

My petite, polite mother started yelling at the man, shaking her finger. Something inside of her summoned up a voice she had never used before and told this man, no matter how intimidating and tall he was, that he was not going to take her baby, her chicle, away.

After I learned this part of the story, whenever I shared it with friends or spoke about it in speeches, I characterized my mom as a feminist American icon who had found her voice. I praised her for understanding her rights before she even had citizenship. The story became about how my mom was a badass who answered back to a man who worked for the government and was many times bigger than her. To me, questioning authority is the true meaning of democracy in action. I relished telling the story and acting it out and giving props to my Mexican mom for being a feminista Chingona badass. People always applauded my mom and her bravery when I finished.

But then, many years later, something happened that changed the way I saw this story. In 2016, one hundred years after Mayor Tom Lea began calling Mexicans "dirty," voters in the United States of America elected a president who told them that Mexicans, immigrants like me, were dangerous. (I'm not going to repeat his words here because, like most of what he has said, they are lies. And I deal in truths, las verdadera verdades.) His words set off a series of ugly policies.

During the forty-fifth president's administration, the distrust and dehumanization of immigrants returned to an all-time high. Beginning in 2017, President Donald Trump, along with Attorney General Jeff Sessions and Senior Policy Advisor

Stephen Miller, devised a "zero tolerance" policy that allowed the US government to respond to the so-called threat of so-called dangerous immigrants by taking away their children. This was people's punishment for trying to come to the US.

Now, you will hear people say things like, *Well, they can't just come here for a better life. They have to stand in line! Do it the right way!* But that's a false narrative. There is NO LINE to stand in or pathway to legal immigration. None. And the waiting list for immigrant visas averages six years to two decades. The idea of coming here "for a better life" sounds nice, but how about this reality: You are starving and you will do anything to help feed your family. Or you are a refugee trying to save your life from oppressive governments, gang violence, or drought and famine caused by the climate crisis. And you have always heard the US describe itself as a welcoming home to immigrants and refugees.

These people are the kings and queens of their homelands, the stars of the movie, the survivors of all time. I would probably be too afraid to leave everything behind like they do, but they make the choice to risk everything so they can live. Don't you want those kinds of human beings as your friends and neighbors?

But by separating people from their children, the US government was saying, *We don't want you here. We don't even want you to think about coming here. So we're going to take away your kids and put them in cages and you may never see them again. That is your punishment for believing the words on the Statue of Liberty. PSYCH!*

Later in 2017, after this policy was in place, a reporter was able to get information from someone who worked inside one of the camps where the children were kept. It was a recording of the children crying inside those cages. The entire world listened to it, including my mother. And that's when our arrival story changed again.

My mother called me after she heard the voices of those babies and kids in American-made cages. She was crying when she said these words: "Mi hijita, it could have been you."

"What?" I asked, not comprehending.

"Mi hijita, it could have been you. Those babies who were taken away from their parents, they tried to do that to *you*."

I sat in shock as I realized the truth. The immigration officer had wanted to take me away from my mom, from my family. Mom said the only reason she screamed at the man was because she went into a state of panic.

"It was the only thing I thought to do," she explained. "I've never screamed in that tone ever before. And it wasn't that I was using my privilege or that I was an American who understood my rights. It was that I was a mother in a state of panic. He wanted to take my child. My new country was welcoming me by threatening to keep my baby."

Now I started crying. In that moment I realized that an experience like this, even when you're not aware it has happened to you, can imprint itself on you like a tattoo.

Once I heard that story, I understood everything about who I am and why I do what I do. I am a proud Mexican immigrant, woman, journalist, and now citizen of the United

States. I have a history in this country. I survived nearly being taken from my mom for no other reason than the fact that I was not born here. But I understand my privilege. That's why I am passing these stories on to you—so that you will keep this history alive and do the work to ask questions about your own history.

CHAPTER 3

Caught Between Two Worlds

Our family's first year in the Windy City of Chicago was a hard transition for all of us. My mom was alone in a cold new city, my sister had left behind her girlfriends and primas, and my two brothers couldn't handle being indoors so much. Outside it was freezing and snowing. None of us had the right jackets and we hadn't yet figured out the trick of layering to stay warm during the winter.

Dad spent his days doing research at the University of Chicago while my sister and brothers began attending Bret Harte Elementary School in our new neighborhood of Hyde Park. That left me with Mom for most of the day, since I wasn't in school yet. Having this private time with her always felt special because I got to see what was going on behind the scenes when everybody else was gone.

Every morning I would watch her shake out the bedsheets, iron them stick straight, and then perfectly remake each of our beds as if no one had ever slept in them. Then my mom would sit down in front of the TV, which back then was so big it was the size of a washing machine, and somebody would come on the screen to do exercises. She followed along and I would try to mimic her and the people on TV.

One of my favorite exercises was when my mom would sit on her butt and crawl forward by moving her butt forward. I would try and do the same thing by using my tiny behind to propel me forward. We both ended up looking pretty silly, like ducks waddling through mud, but I remember laughing a lot with my mother whenever she was doing these workouts.

One day, the exercise show was suddenly interrupted. A white man with white hair and a mustache appeared on the screen. He said in English that President John F. Kennedy had been shot. I didn't understand exactly what that meant, but I remember turning to my mother and watching her break down in tears. I had never seen her cry before and it was very scary. She had always been the one who comforted me when I cried, so seeing her like that, I didn't know what to do. I gave her a hug.

This was the first time a journalist delivering the news on television made an impression on me—and on so many levels. He was delivering breaking news right after the event had happened; he was finding a way to speak about a tragedy; he was documenting history. I later learned the man with the white hair was Walter Cronkite.

I was beginning to understand that journalists told us about what was happening in this country. Everybody who had a television or a radio on November 22, 1963, was listening to

Walter Cronkite as he delivered the fateful news about JFK's assassination. The news brought us together as a country, in a way, because it made us realize we were witnessing our collective history even though the country was very divided.

At the end of that year, my father was invited to do a residency at Harvard University. Once again our family uprooted itself to embark on a new adventure for the sake of my dad's microscope in an equally chilly city called Brookline that was just outside Boston, Massachusetts.

One of my first memories is of the two-story house we lived in there, which was provided by the university and located in a neighborhood called Coolidge Corner.

My brothers and sister and I felt safe and warm inside the Brookline house, although sometimes it felt a little peculiar because it was furnished with things that didn't belong to us. The only traumatic moment was when my brother Jorge accidentally killed his pet hamster by squeezing and hugging him to death. He loved him too much and didn't realize he was hurting him.

Mom carried me around on her hip almost everywhere in that old wooden house. For me, at three years old, mi vida was good. My dad was at work all day and sometimes on weekends too, which left mom at home alone with four young children in a strange city in a strange country. Everyone she knew and loved outside of Dad and us kids was thousands of miles away in Mexico. She was having such a hard time, feeling so lonely and overwhelmed, that it was decided my grandfather, grandmother, aunt, uncle, and his wife would all come to visit us in Brookline. It became a big family trip to visit the little sister who had left Mexico and moved to the United States. It was also an important pep-talk moment for my mom, because she needed help and encouragement.

In addition, my grandfather helped pay for a young woman named Isabel to come from Mexico and be my mother's helper. I remember Isabel's warm arms wrapped around me, her dark, curly hair, and her smile that looked like the sun shining. Mom later told me this visit from her family was one of the things that helped save her life, reminded her where she came from, and gave her a sense of hope that she needed as she made her way in a new country.

The house was filled with people speaking Spanish and in the kitchen women were making the dishes that we used to eat at our weekly comidas del mediodía. One day we all gathered outside on the steps in front of our house for an impromptu family portrait—me and Jorge in the front, my uncle on the left with my grandmother and Isabel behind him; my two aunts in the middle have pink rollers in their hair, while my mom stands next to them; and my grandfather is on the far right with a cigarette dangling out of his mouth.

My abuelito, of course, arrived with gifts for us, including a big, mysterious-looking box called a record player. My sister, who was ten, quickly lost interest after playing with it a few times and my brothers were busy playing outside. So I sat by myself on the floor with this box.

The record player came with a book and one six-inch record. When I flipped through the book, the world inside was painted in pink and lavender and pastel green. It looked like a candy shop, where everything you saw was edible. I wanted to lick the pages like a lollipop. The drawings of people in festive red and white outfits and colorful horses on a carousel told a story about a fantasy land where people danced and sang all the time.

Unlike the rainbow world inside the book, the streets outside our house in Brookline were cold and gray, and the trees turned into sad, brown skeletons after they lost all their leaves in winter. Just looking at the book transported me to another world.

At the back of the book on the last page was an envelope with a record inside. I would slide out the record, which looked like a thick, black plastic disc, open the box with the record player, and then lay the disc down on top by lining up the hole in the center of the disc with the short metal post sticking out on top of the player. Then I moved the arm onto the record disc, which was already spinning. At first it made a scratching sound, but then suddenly I would hear music and the voices of the characters from the book.

The people who rode around on carousel horses in the pastel-colored land sang a song together, and in the song was a word that I had never heard before. SOO-PER-CALLA-something-something. I couldn't make out the rest. To me, this word represented everything about the language that was not being spoken inside my house, the language I heard only when I stepped outside. I didn't speak English, but I didn't really know many words in either language yet.

It took me a long time to figure out how to even pronounce the word. I listened to that box playing the record over and over again all by myself behind a door in the other room where there was an outlet in the wall. Everyone was busy in the kitchen telling stories, cooking, listening to my grandfather, and laughing. No one worried or came looking for me because they knew I was safe in the house and they probably heard the record repeating endlessly.

Can you imagine being three years old and trying to learn one of the hardest words to say in the English language, which also happens to be a language you don't speak? As I listened to the record, I followed along in the book and sounded out the letters that made up the word. Eventually, somehow, I did it.

SUPER-CALI-FRAGI-LISTIC-EXPI-ALI-DOCIOUS. Supercalifragilisticexpialidocious!

Maybe that was the beginning of me challenging myself to stretch outside my comfort zone, to conquer things that didn't quite make sense to me yet. It's also possible that I was beginning to understand that there were certain things I needed to know to navigate the world outside of our house.

It wasn't long after my family's visit from Mexico and the magical record player with its Mary Poppins wonderland that my dad completed his residency at Harvard and we packed up and returned to Chicago.

The Civil Rights era was in full swing, and even at the young age of four I was picking up on the anguish and frustration in the air. In Chicago, we lived in a neighborhood of white and Black families, store owners, police officers, teachers, and librarians who were all living their lives together. Yet on the TV screen every night we watched white protestors and police harassing and beating Black people. I didn't understand why this was happening. I watched policemen aim powerful fire hoses at Black people who were beautifully dressed in crisp button-down shirts, freshly ironed slacks, and leather shoes for the men; lady-like dresses and flawlessly curled hair for the women.

I didn't know it at the time, but dressing to the nines was actually a tactic of Black protestors. Because white people in positions of authority unfairly held them to a higher standard—using a Black person's stray hair or untucked shirt as an excuse to call into question their respectability—activists made a point of presenting themselves in a way that was beyond reproach. So why were they still being hosed? Why were the police letting their vicious German Shepherds loose to attack them?

I already knew that something was amiss in this place that was now my home, where we spoke Spanish in the house and another language outside. I was happy in this place, but there was something wrong. It had to do with people who were darker-skinned and the white people who hated them because of it.

Many years later, around 2010, when my dad was sick with Alzheimer's, my family and I started going through boxes of his love letters to my mother from when he had traveled to the United States by bus for the first time in the mid-1950s.

Dad had never told us the story of his arrival, probably because it was painful for him to remember. But learning the story from his letters helped me understand so much about my father and those of us who live in the United States but were not born here.

Several years before he was hired by the University of Chicago, my dad traveled there for a job interview. He took a bus from Mexico to Chicago because he couldn't afford a plane ticket. On the bus ride he watched the scenery as they crossed the US-Mexico border into Texas. The landscape was all flat brown land as far as the eye could see under a hot, burning sun. After several miles, they made their first pit stop in Texas.

In the letter, he wrote about what happened when he got off there to use the bathroom. He walked to the men's room and learned he had to make a choice. There were two doors and a sign above each. One sign was labeled "White" and the other said "Colored." Dad was very confused. He didn't understand what this meant. The US was supposed to be more advanced than Mexico. How was it that they had two bathrooms based on the color of your skin?

This was during the 1950s and segregation was still alive and well in the South. Segregation was a policy based on the idea that Black people and white people should have "separate but equal" facilities for all kinds of things like schools, buses, movie theaters, water fountains, and even bathrooms. But the very idea of needing to separate people based on their color or their race is inherently unequal. White politicians passed laws that created and maintained segregation, motivated by hatred, racism, and the desire to make Black people feel less than them.

Standing outside the two doors to the men's restroom, my dad looked at his skin. It wasn't really white and it wasn't really black. It had more color than white, and yet it wasn't black.

He knew that apart from the amount of melanin in the epidermis, the medical term for skin, there was no difference between people's bodies. He knew that because he had done surgery.

Now he was faced with making a very unscientific decision. In the end, he chose to walk through the door labeled "White." He chose privilege, he chose to pass, and that's what made this memory so painful. In choosing to pass for white, he understood that he was invisible in the US as a Mexican.

Clearly, Americans saw things only in black and white, and they didn't want those two things to mix together. Where was his place in America as a Brown man who speaks Spanish? If they could do this to Black people, couldn't they also do it to people like him?

My father understood from the moment he stepped into the United States that division based on race was a deep, deep part of this country. He realized he was not going to be able to solve this problem, and I think that made him feel a little distrustful. It is hard to love a place when you're not exactly sure where you fit in or if you'll ever truly be accepted there.

As a child in Chicago, I didn't know this story about my dad. I was just a little girl finding love and warmth and Mexico inside our apartment. But outside in the cold, where I watched the anger boil against peaceful protesters, I was trying to understand how love and hate could exist in the same place and time. Was America really the place for us? Was this really going to be our home?

CHAPTER 4

Being Different in Hyde Park

Our neighborhood of Hyde Park on the South Side of Chicago was different from most other places. We were quirky Hyde Parkers. We didn't use words like "diverse" or "minorities," but our neighborhood was essentially a model for multiculturalism. Hyde Park was the only place in the entire city of Chicago where Black and white people lived together. Living there made me think it was cool to be different.

We all liked being different. Maybe it was because our neighborhood was right next to Lake Michigan and that made us feel freer to be who we wanted to be, because we didn't feel boxed in. Maybe it was because the University of Chicago attracted people from all over the world who didn't carry the same racism in their bones, the way the people of the United States have historically. Maybe it was because of the great migration of Black people from the South to the North and

Midwest, and that strong sense of family that many Black people brought with them.

In fact, the day my mom walked in with her four kids to register us for school, the principal and other administrators applauded because they were so excited to have new students from Mexico. Imagine being applauded for being Mexican immigrants in your school!

My mom walked my sister and brothers to school most days, and since I was her chicle, I always went along too. On those walks to school we got to know Lorraine, the crossing guard. Lorraine wore a white hat that looked like a pilot's cap, white gloves, and about four or five layers to keep her warm under her black crossing guard coat that stretched almost to the ground. She was under five feet tall.

Lorraine was originally from the South, so "good morning" just rolled off her tongue. *Good morning, honey. Good morning, sweetie. Good morning, baby. Have a beautiful day.* Lorraine gave hugs, and I was a kid who grew up giving and getting hugs. That came from my mom and her very Mexican way of being a Mexican mom. So I hugged Lorraine every morning.

Soon my mom and Lorraine were chit-chatting—Lorraine with her slow Southern drawl from Mississippi and my mom with her thick Mexican accent. They became close friends and Lorraine started coming over to hang out at our apartment to pass the time between her shifts. Sometimes she helped my mom clean the house. This helped my mom but it also helped Rain, as we called her, because she didn't have to find a warm place to stay between the morning, lunch, and after-school shifts.

They spent many, many days like this together and we all loved Rain in de Face, which is the nickname she gave herself. Even though my dad was very serious and quite distant, Lorraine started to call him "darling" to poke fun at how solemn and deep in thought he usually was. They, too, became friends, though with very few words. Lorraine became part of our family.

We had been in the United States for maybe five years at this point. Thanksgiving was an unfamiliar tradition to us as Mexicans, and we were still learning what it was all about. I didn't quite believe the story we were told about the pilgrims and Indigenous people being all lovey dovey.

One year Lorraine invited us to Thanksgiving at her house. My dad dropped us off on his way to work, because he loved to work and he wasn't a big holiday guy anyway. That was when my mom realized the address Lorraine had given us was at a housing project where poor families had been forced to live after being displaced in their own communities, or sometimes it was the only place a recently arrived migrant from the South could afford to live.

My mom and dad were not judgmental about things like this. Everything about the United States was still new and interesting and curious to them. They also weren't carrying around ingrained ideas of racism or elitism that said you can't go celebrate Thanksgiving in a housing project on the South Side of Chicago where the white folks did not go because they thought it was unsafe (which is another way that racism shows up).

The building felt cold, like touching stainless steel in the middle of winter. There was probably no heat in the elevator or in the hallways, though there were a lot of apartments on every floor. Lorraine's apartment was tiny but it smelled like delicious turkey. There were dishes I had never seen before that she identified as collard greens and candied yams. We sat around Lorraine's linoleum table with her daughter and ate turkey drumsticks together.

It was the smell and taste of Lorraine's turkey that finally persuaded my mom to start celebrating Thanksgiving at our house and to make her own turkey. That's how good it was. We had ice cream for dessert, and after that, Lorraine took out her boxing gloves. She showed us how to fight and make a right hook. She let us try on her leather gloves and they were so heavy. As a crossing guard, Lorraine was all, *Oh honey* this, *Oh sugar* that, but that night I learned that you should never cross her.

That same year, I started kindergarten at Bret Harte Elementary School. I was the happiest person in our family, along with my mother, who finally was going to have some peace during the day. Because I was the youngest of four children, I always wanted to do what my older siblings were doing. I loved being my mother's chicle, but I was also kind of done with it. I wanted to be a big kid and, at five years old, it was finally my chance.

Bret Harte Elementary was named after the writer and poet Bret Harte, who wrote about his experiences on the frontier and the Gold Rush in California. The poem that made him famous, first published in 1870, was called "Plain Language from Truthful James," but most people came to know it as "The Heathen Chinee." Even though Harte's intention was to criticize the violence Irish immigrants used against Chinese immigrants, the poem ended up fueling anti-Chinese sentiment among the white working class. By 1882, the US government passed the Chinese Exclusion Act, which banned the immigration of all Chinese laborers. I didn't know this when I was five years old, but when I learned who Bret Harte was many years later, it gave me pause to think about all the kids who have walked under his name every morning and afternoon. Pay attention to who your community chooses to honor with statues, monuments, plaques, and named buildings.

Our school building reminded me of a castle. It was made of red brick and the entrance was enclosed inside a square turret, also brick, that looked like a small tower. You entered by walking up a regal set of stairs and turning left into the turret and through the double doors that were made of wood and heavy glass. As a little girl, the proportions of everything felt huge to me. The desks were big, the chairs were big, the hallways were big. The eighth graders were enormous.

I was the shortest kid in my grade, which was made up of the youngest students, so basically, I was the smallest kid in the entire school. I was afraid and nervous on that first day, like every other kid, but what added to my fear was not really knowing what to do about speaking one language at school and another language inside my home. What was up with that?

I didn't understand why my life at school and home felt so different. Apart from my siblings, there weren't any other students in my entire grammar school who spoke Spanish—at least none that I knew of. I had a card at home that said I was an "alien." Often, because I spoke another language and had parents who spoke with thick accents, I did feel like an alien. Our house smelled different, the music was in Spanish, we were loud, and none of us was blond.

No one at school purposely made me feel that way. Bret Harte was that kind of school. Everybody from Hyde Park attended the public schools and everybody did their best to get along, but sometimes there were fights after school. The fights didn't fall along racial lines. They were about jealous boys or angry girls fighting over a boy. That kind of trivial stuff. No one carried weapons back then. Never, not to a grammar school.

In addition to fights, there was one other thing I was afraid of. It was the mid-1960s, about twenty years after World War II when the world took on the Nazis. It had also been twenty years since Japan had bombed Pearl Harbor and then the US dropped the atom bomb on Hiroshima and Nagasaki. President Harry Truman's decision to use the A-bomb on other human beings, even in a time of war, was a horrific human rights violation on a massive scale.

The generations of people who had lived through the war were still in a state of post-trauma. We didn't have a name for it like they do now: PTSD or post-traumatic stress disorder. Now we talk about how this can happen to people who serve in a war or are on the front lines. In the late 1960s, World War II had ended only twenty years earlier and Jewish survivors of the Nazis and concentration/death camps were around us in real life. Later, I would be told that the reason Mr. and Mrs. Tannenbaum, who owned the corner five and dime store called Tannebaum's, always wore long sleeves, even in the 100 percent humidity of a Chicago summer, was because they had both been tattooed when Nazis put them into a death camp in Europe.

So the possibility of another world war was, like, for real. To cope with the stress and fear of a future bombing, many schools still conducted air raid drills. All my classmates and I knew was that when a certain bell sounded, we were supposed to line up in our classroom and then march in a single file down the stairwell. Once all the kindergarteners were there, we put our heads underneath our folded arms while we rested them up against a wall. In the world's most advanced nation, which had already dropped an atom bomb on another country, that was the best they could do to protect us at school. Thankfully, no air raids or bombings ever happened during my elementary school days.

No, if anything, school was safe. It was a place of friendship, reading, and community. My favorite teacher was Mrs. Lois Turner, who taught my first-grade class. She was the first Black teacher I had and one of the sweetest, kindest human beings I ever met. Mrs. Turner saw me. She understood that while I loved being in school, I struggled because I was the runt of the pack. English was still my second language. I had hair like no one else. If I didn't wear a stocking over my hair, then it would be wild, curly, and poofy—the opposite of the straight blond that was held up as the ideal in movies, TV, and advertisements.

She made a point of calling on me in class, and that motivated me to raise my hand more, because I wanted her to see me. She embodied warmth, tenderness, and patience. To the boys in our class who tried to act out, though, she was stern. I did not want to get that look from Mrs. Turner.

Mrs. Turner was a proud Black woman who led with her humanity and, in the process, taught us all how to do the same. While people were protesting and demanding their civil rights in the streets of the South Side of Chicago, just blocks from our school, Mrs. Turner taught us to sing Irish folk songs and had us read about characters like Dick and Jane, who lived in places that looked nothing like our city's neighborhoods. Her classroom was also where we studied Thor Heyerdahl, an explorer and ethnographer who traveled the world and wanted to make a point about human migration. He believed that the oceans between continents were not dividing us, but uniting us. Heyerdahl, a Norwegian man, couldn't have been more different from me, a Mexican girl living in Chicago, but with Mrs. Turner, we tracked his sea voyage every day in class.

The 1960s was an era of overturning outdated and biased beliefs and policies. Bret Harte Elementary, like many schools at the time, clung to certain traditions that were quite backward. For instance, it was against the school dress code for girls to wear pants. That's right, administrators were forbidding girls from wearing pants to school.

You may know what it's like to experience winter in Chicago, but if you don't, let me just say it's really, really freaking cold. Twenty-five degrees Fahrenheit cold. So cold that your snot freezes and it feels like you have a bunch of little icicles in your nose. I did not enjoy going to school wearing dresses and skirts in below-freezing temperatures, but that's how it was way back then.

Some of the feminist mothers started talking about this absurd rule and how it essentially oppressed and controlled girls. Since it was a time when everybody was questioning everything, kind of like what happened with the horrors and inequalities borne out by the COVID-19 pandemic and the Black Lives Matter protests in 2020, the feminist moms, including my own, decided to start a petition to get Bret Harte's principal and staff to remove the ban on girls wearing pants. While they were still dialoguing with the school administration about the ban, we started wearing pants under our skirts. It kept us warm and it was an interesting style, but we really just wanted to wear pants. Eventually, almost all the girls started wearing pants like this. The moms kept up their pressure with petitions and the school's leaders relented. We broke the patriarchy! Girls were officially allowed to wear pants to school and I learned a lesson about holding the powerful to account (even when it's just the principal of your elementary school).

Living in Hyde Park and going to Bret Harte gave me the chance to make new friends and hang out at their homes. These visits opened my eyes to other realities and ways of living. It taught me that although where we lived may have looked different, smaller, bigger, more or less organized, as people we were all essentially the same. The aromas of every household were different and delicious and particular, and no one's smell was better than the rest.

I loved bopping around to different people's houses and playing with my friends. These mini adventures helped me to sharpen my powers of observation as a future journalist. At Elizabeth's house I ate bagels and lox for the first time in my life. My friend Emmett had light skin, a light brown Afro, and a deep voice that used to make us all laugh when he imitated Scooby-Doo. Teresa, who was Black, invited me to her house where we danced the Grandpa to The Jackson 5. There was Derek, who was cute with a roundish belly and a close-cropped Afro who often wore his Boy Scout uniform to school. At Susie's house I played with the Barbie dolls she got for Hanukkah. My friend Charlie Moy's parents owned the Chinese restaurant on the corner where everybody ate. Mary was Japanese American and at her house we made sugar cookies.

Some of my friends lived in big apartments on the top floor with four bedrooms and long hallways. Others lived in houses. And some of my friends lived a little bit farther away in housing projects like Lorraine's. But Hyde Park was home to all types of people, so I got to be friends with everybody and I saw how everybody lived.

I got to know everybody's family history, too—and, through that, learn more about my adopted country, the good and the bad. My friend Elizabeth had a white mom who was from West Virginia and a father who was Japanese American. Her father's family had survived something commonly called the Japanese Internment. But that innocuous-sounding name covers something horrible our government perpetrated against its own people.

During World War II, the US government imprisoned Japanese Americans, half of whom were children, in camps far away from their homes, in some cases for as long as four years. These were American citizens. Many of them lost businesses and homes they had worked hard to build. The government's lawmakers believed that Japanese Americans couldn't be trusted after Japan's military attacked Pearl Harbor, but they never locked up German Americans or Italian Americans, even though we were fighting Germany and Italy at the same time.

Remember when I said words have power? How we define things matters. It's the difference between calling something the "Japanese Internment" versus what it really was, the imprisonment of innocent American citizens because they had Japanese ancestry. When we use words that accurately describe what the government did to this group of Americans, the injustice is impossible to ignore. Think carefully about the terms you use when you're referring to people and moments in history. Elizabeth's family's story revealed a side of the United States that I hadn't known about before, and changed the way I saw the world.

And the world was changing around me, too. In the city of Chicago and across the country, people were rising up, some to fight injustices, some to preserve them. Every day brought a new protest—against the war in Vietnam, for women's liberation, to end poverty. And whenever college and high school students came out to peacefully protest against the war, police showed up in riot gear to meet them with billy clubs, tear gas, and a lot of violence.

We sometimes used to pass by a cement underpass beneath the train tracks on weekend outings. It was there I saw the words "Who killed Fred Hampton?" graffitied in black spray paint. I was eight years old and didn't know who Fred Hampton was, but I knew that somebody had killed him and that people had questions about it that weren't being answered. Many years later I learned that Fred Hampton was a young activist and chairman of the Black Panther Party in Illinois; he was just twenty-one when the FBI shot him dead in 1969.

During the 1960s and '70s, we didn't call police officers "police officers." We called them "pigs." The television was constantly replaying images of white police officers wearing helmets, taking out billy clubs, and hitting teenagers and young people over their heads until blood poured out. Politicians and movement leaders were being assassinated regularly. In a span of five years, we lost John F. Kennedy, Medgar Evers, Malcolm X, Martin Luther King Jr., and Robert F. Kennedy. I watched college students at Kent State University get murdered by the police for protesting the Vietnam War. I didn't know that what I was witnessing was a country fighting for its soul and its democracy.

When I was around four years old, I saw the Reverend Martin Luther King Jr., a Black minister and civil rights leader, speak on television for the first time. He spoke eloquently and powerfully; he knew how to make people feel things when he spoke. He told us not to judge a person "by the color of their skin, but by the content of their character."

When you're a Mexican kid growing up without a whole lot

of other kids who look like you, someone like Martin Luther King Jr. stating that we are all part of this country and that we all deserve a voice and to be treated equally touches you. He reminded me of my uncles. He was a bit darker, but he had the same mustache, the same bald head, the same kind eyes, beautiful full lips, and smile. He also said that love needed to be the force that pushed people forward. That notion appealed to me. There was always a lot of love in my family, so why not move with love?

Even though I hadn't been born in this country, and even though I had a Mexican passport, Martin Luther King Jr. was the first person to ever make me feel like maybe one day there was a possibility that I, too, could become an American. But even if I didn't feel American yet, I felt like a citizen of Hyde Park.

My neighborhood was a small world where I was beginning to fit in like the missing piece of a puzzle. But soon a new experience would show me how I might start to make other parts of this gray city feel like home as well.

Dad bought a car.

CHAPTER 5

Invisible Borders

Now that we had wheels, my weekdays were busy with going to school and hanging out with my new friends in Hyde Park. But weekends were spent in Pilsen with my parents. The neighborhood of Pilsen, more than thirty blocks northwest of Hyde Park, was the heart of El Barrio Mexicano in Chicago. Although we had a local cooperative supermarket in our neighborhood where Mom bought staples like cereal, canned goods, and bread, on the weekends she and my dad and me (I was still too young to leave behind with my brothers and sister) would drive over to Pilsen for the primary grocery shopping, where I inhaled the smell of warm chicharrón and the familiar sights and sounds of Mexican culture.

Chicago is a city that has been defined by racism and segregation. Everyone knew where the borders for their neighborhood were, and they knew not to cross them. If you were Polish, you stayed in Bridgeport, the Polish neighborhood. If you were from the Ukraine, you stayed in the Ukrainian Village area. If you were Black, you stayed in Black neighborhoods like South Shore or Garfield Park. If you were Mexican, you stayed around 18th Street in Pilsen. Diez y ocho.

The car ride itself was a kind of passage from the multiculti, majority Black and Jewish neighborhood of Hyde Park where everybody looked different from one another to a neighborhood where Spanish was spoken everywhere. And I mean every-where—on the streets, in the stores, in the beauty salons, and on the buses. To get to 18th Street, my dad would drive us up Lake Shore Drive in his long, green station wagon that looked like an alligator.

On the ride there we passed a series of massive buildings that were gray and ugly—public housing projects like the one Lorraine lived in. Even though the buildings were right next to Lake Michigan, with its beautiful turquoise and golden colors, all the windows faced the opposite side. The people living in the apartments couldn't even look out onto the lake and enjoy the view. Nearly everyone who lived in the housing projects was a Black Chicagoan.

Once we left Hyde Park and the South Side of the city, we almost completely stopped seeing Black people. You might see some Black people working downtown along State Street or Michigan Avenue, but there were no residential neighbor-hoods on the North Side where Black people lived. As a child, I didn't know that there was a racist policy behind this called redlining, which gave politicians the power to divide up city neighborhoods based on a color-coded system. Housing agencies run by the federal government drew red lines on maps around what they considered "undesirable" neighborhoods to indicate that they were high risk for insurance and lending banks. But usually, the only criteria for redlining a neighborhood were race and income. Without investment and other resources, these communities, which were mainly comprised of Black and Brown people, were left to fend for themselves. This is how white supremacy affected housing in one of the country's most important cities, and you can still see its legacy in Chicago and many other US cities today, nearly a century after the government first created redlining.

My dad would usually turn at McCormick Place and we'd speed past a giant warehouse and convention center into an industrial part of Chicago on the West Side. We drove through a few underpasses, made a final exit off to the left, and then landed on 18th Street.

Pilsen didn't look like any other part of Chicago I knew. It was drab gray, almost lifeless, and the curtains and blinds in all the windows were drawn. The apartment buildings were dark and squat with only one or two stories.

I found this perplexing. Why were the streets in Hyde Park so broad and clean, while the streets of Pilsen were dirty and littered with garbage? Why were broken windows boarded up instead of being fixed? Why did one of the only playgrounds for the entire community have a rusted, old jungle gym? And why did everyone who looked and sounded like us live here?

I didn't understand then that the litter, uncared-for buildings, and lack of safe playgrounds were all symptoms of exclusion and deprivation motivated by racism. The city government's lawmakers had made the decision to abandon a community: El Barrio Mexicano. These civic leaders had decided that "those people" didn't need clean streets or streetlights because they saw Mexicans and Mexican Americans as less than human. This allowed them to justify the inequality and keep the resources where they wanted them: in the white neighborhoods whose votes they most cared about. This is where you learn that getting involved sometimes looks like voting, because you can use it to vote out the politicians who don't represent you. Other times getting involved looks like protesting or calling your congressperson.

After my dad found a parking spot, we'd walk into the grocery store and the smell of chicharrón enveloped everything in its path. It was like a superhero putting a freeze on you so that your whole body was surrounded in ice, only in my case the ice was the dark and crunchy scent of chicharrón.

The grocery store was the first place my mother let me explore on my own, to keep me occupied while she got her shopping done. They kept the chicharrón in a glass box heated with light bulbs. I would walk over to the man behind the butcher counter, who had a belly and wore a white apron, and ask for a crispy piece of the deep-fried pig skin. He would smile and reach into the glass box with his tongs and pull out a crunchy piece to hand me. That always made me happy.

Sometimes I'd wander up and down the grocery aisles, looking at the packages of food with words I couldn't read because they were in Spanish (eventually I taught myself how to read in Spanish by studying comic books). Unlike the neighborhood's gloomy exterior, inside the market all I saw was color, color, and more color. There were jars and cans filled with sauces and fruits and vegetables, including red, yellow, and green chilies; bags of dried bay leaves, oregano, and whole cinnamon sticks; galletas Marias and dulces de tamarindo; tortillas of every kind, corn and flour. These were things I had never seen anywhere outside of Mexico, let alone at our coop supermarket in Hyde Park. In Chicago, they could only be found on 18th Street.

When my mom walked in here, she was a queen. Everybody greeted her. *Ay, Señora, como le va. Que le damos, que quiere usted?* They spoke to her using the formal form of "you," which I rarely heard because the people I spoke Spanish with were my family and we were always informal.

Everyone at the grocery store was thrilled to see my mother. Often Dad waited in the car while we shopped, either because he would get bored and antsy, or maybe because he knew this was a sphere where my mother reigned supreme. Perhaps he wanted to let her be the queen, but it also might have made him a little bit jealous to watch all the men flirting and chatting up Mom. *Que bonita se ve, señora. Que linda sonrisa tiene hoy, señora!*

For me it was pure fun to watch the men behind the counters interact with my petite mom, dressed up in her heels and cat eye makeup. She would place her order and say, "Give me twelve thin sliced bistec, tres libras de puerco. . . ." She always bought a lot of meat because there were six of us and there was a lot of meat-eating going on. The way my mom was raised, eating meat was a symbol of privilege.

Mom also bought there the canned salsas we ate—Salsa Herdez or Valentina or chile chipotle. Most people had no idea what chipotle was back then, but my mom was buying cans of chipotle the color of burnt brick. The gooey, reddish peppers inside were intriguing to me as a little girl and even a little gross. I had never seen food that color in the United States. Whenever I tried a bite of the chipotles, my mouth stung like crazy. To be honest, I was scared of chili chipotle. I knew to stay away from it, but at the same time I dreamed of one day being able to put it in my tacos and sandwiches the way my mom did.

Our last stop was the tortilleria next door, a separate shop and small factory where we would pick up dozens of fresh tortillas, just the way they made them in Mexico. I could ask for one of them to be taken out of the paper wrapper, still warm, and I'd roll it up between my hands and eat it just like that.

Our weekend trips from Hyde Park to Pilsen were one of many experiences I had early on as someone who crosses borders. I began to witness, though I didn't yet understand, the borders that people have made between neighborhoods, between people. My mom and dad, it seemed, were able to float in and out of these bordered places because they didn't want to be a part of the racism that was all around us. They had crossed one border already, so to them, borders were meant to be crossed even if it felt scary. We went downtown. We went to the North Side where my dad's doctor friends lived. We went to the deep South Side down 63rd Street where people on the loud elevated trains stared down on us from above. When we went to Midway Airport to pick up a visiting tio or prima, we went through Cicero, where I had seen TV reports of screaming white people protesting with signs that said Black people were not welcome there. We went to Pilsen where everyone spoke Spanish.

Somehow we were able to come and go from these places, but we didn't see anyone else crossing these invisible borders. I never saw one white person in Pilsen, and not one Mexican on the North Side. These experiences left a mark on my heart and my mind. Today I am still a border crosser. As a journalist I am always going into new places, trying to find people and stories and communities where other people haven't wanted to go in the past or where they think they don't belong.

I was learning at that young age, from the grocery store to the tortilleria to the carniceria to the tailor, that there was a whole other life in Pilsen that was completely Mexican. I loved that I could be there and at the same time be so close to my home in Hyde Park. Still, it bothered me that the two neighborhoods I loved most in my city looked nothing alike. Why did they look so different when, at the heart, they were the same?

CHAPTER 6

This Is What Democracy Looks Like

ᦲᦲᦲ

Pilsen and El Barrio Mexicano felt like home. Warm. Acogedor, which means welcoming. School often felt that way too. Except for one moment that stands out.

In third grade I had my first experience with a mean teacher. Mrs. Jaye had reddish orange hair that she wore in thick curls on either side of her head, which made her look a little bit like a mushroom top. Mrs. Jaye was very tall. She wore skirts that were big and poofy and looked like they had petticoats underneath. She always wore a white, button-down dress shirt and a skirt secured at her waist with a belt, as if she was still in the 1950s. In reality, it was the end of the 1960s and women were burning their bras as an act of public feminism.

Mrs. Jaye was the opposite of Mrs. Turner. Where Mrs. Turner was warm and inviting and always offering me a hug, Mrs. Jaye was like a refrigerator—and you cannot hug a refrigerator. She also had her own private bathroom inside the classroom off a side door and that made us kids squeamish. When she blew her nose in there it sounded like a loud, long fart.

One day we heard that there was going to be a demonstration in our own neighborhood in support of the Civil Rights movement and Martin Luther King Jr. What I didn't know was that Bertha Elena—the firstborn, the daughter who was under my father's watchful eye at all times, the girl who was always dressed in high style and was voted best physique in the entire high school—had already become the young social activist of our family. She was the one who first brought those values and beliefs into our home. Now my mom decided that she had to show up for the cause, and if she was going to the protest, then she was going to take me and my siblings with her.

Demonstrations like these during the 1960s built the foundation for what we know today as the Black Lives Matter movement. This protest was part of the long struggle for justice for Black people in the United States, which in my view started the day the first enslaved person was brought to this land in 1619. And being able to exercise your First Amendment right to freedom of speech by protesting in the streets has been a central part of American history since the American Revolution.

People who cared about civil rights and equality knew that it was important to show up and support this demonstration. My mother, along with several other mothers, decided to pull me and my siblings from school so that we could go and witness the event. Those of us who had cool parents brought letters to our teachers to excuse our absence. I delivered mine to Mrs. Jaye, who read it with a scoff.

I don't remember whether Mrs. Jaye spoke to me, but her knitted eyebrows and frowning lips said it all. She clearly did not approve of a student missing a day of school to go to a civil rights demonstration. What she didn't understand was that experiencing an event like that out in the world would teach me so much more than I ever could have learned reading about it in her class.

The day my mom took us to the protest was a pivotal moment in our family. My sister's activism, and therefore all of ours, now had the stamp of approval from the woman who ran our home, or as we say in Spanish, la que maneja la casa, the one who drives the house. The chauffeur of the household was teaching us that protest was an all-American tradition.

My father, on the other hand, did not like the idea of his wife and his children attending a protest rally and being absorbed into a crowd of people where anything could happen. A number of people had been shot at protests and hundreds had been beaten up, tear-gassed, and arrested by the police. On some level, I believe my dad came to internalize many of the anti-Black sentiments that are regularly repeated in the media. He was the guy who bought into the stereotype that a Black man on the street could be dangerous. We got a sense, whether he said it outright or not, that he felt joining a protest where the majority of the people were Black might not be right for his family.

A person may hold racist or prejudiced beliefs because they have been raised with them and encouraged to accept them as truth, and because they hear those beliefs repeated over and over. In my father's case, even though he had been treated badly for being a Mexican and had experienced anti-Blackness and hated it, the media fed him with stories that said Black people were a problem. This kind of racism is learned and ingrained, but it doesn't have to be permanent. Soon enough, Dad would meet his future BFF on the South Side of Chicago, far from his hometown of Tampico. He was a distinguished Black man named Jerry Morgan, and the two of them became lifelong friends. Thankfully, Papi did not die clinging to those racist beliefs.

I didn't hear my parents fight over the rally, but I knew that there was a division in our household related to it. My mom also ignored some white friends who told her she was being an irresponsible mother by exposing herself and her kids to the possibility of getting shot. From my point of view, it was pretty cool that my mom wanted to participate in a protest.

The protest was held in the middle of the day and was crowded with mostly Black folks and white allies. The overall theme was in support of civil rights, but we marched and chanted specifically against housing discrimination and redlining. Mom was beaming with excitement and thrilled to be there.

I felt small among so many adults, but the passion was energizing. The people who spoke at the rally were larger than life. Jesse Jackson was there with his big Afro. People had made signs out of cardboard boxes and sticks. Some people had bells. Others just had their anger and their voices. Being at the protest and participating along with everyone else was a life-changing moment, like being hit by lightning.

"No war! We want peace!" everybody was chanting in unison. *This is what democracy feels like,* I thought. And I liked it. I liked the collective energy of everybody banding together in solidarity. Being there was uplifting. My heart felt as if it might burst, but in a good way, like a flower blooming in a slow, beautiful unfurling. Despite my fears that the demonstration might turn to violence and anger, my heart was opening up to this experience of protest. I felt a real sense of trust in the crowd, a reassurance that they had my back, which was something I had never felt before. I felt happy, included, and encouraged. I felt heard.

I was not a US citizen yet. Even so, I realized that you don't have to be a citizen to take part in democracy and that going to a protest is what people do in the United States. Marching in the street, peacefully but forcefully, is how we express our views on important issues and it's also our democratic right.

I was beginning to like politics and to understand that it wasn't merely something to watch on a television screen, but something I could participate in. I fell in love with using my voice, a loud one at that, and it felt good to be screaming and yelling for what I knew was right. Dr. Martin Luther King Jr. stood for love and compassion. On the opposite side it was so clear there was only hate.

Protests were covered on television almost every single night in 1968. My childhood in this country as an immigrant was imbued with the anger that Americans felt toward one another. There were Black Power demonstrations against systemic racism and women burning their bras in garbage cans in defiance of the patriarchy. There were peace protests on college campuses objecting to the war in Vietnam; protests outside the Democratic National Convention in 1968; and white-only protests and Nazi rallies. Even the Beatles, the biggest rock and roll band of the era in the US despite being British, were all about protest, from their mop-top haircuts to their refusal to play for segregated audiences.

I heard a lot of screaming and chanting as a little girl. It worried and scared me. When you see police in riot gear beating protesters over the head with billy clubs simply for exercising their right to free speech, of course you're going to be worried about protests. You're going to think that's how they all end—in violence.

So it wasn't until my mom decided to take me and my brothers and sister to the rally in support of the Civil Rights movement that my perception of protests changed. The idea of a political rally, like the ones I had seen on television with tens of thousands of people, taking place in my small neighborhood seemed like the biggest thing that could ever possibly happen there.

Up to that point, my siblings and I were never allowed to miss a school day, not ever, ever, ever, unless we had a fever. My mother's decision to take us out of school had something to do with her newfound friends. They were other mothers, white, Black, Asian, and Jewish women in Hyde Park. In the mornings after they dropped off their kids at school, many of them would socialize and talk about the politics of the moment. My mom was getting educated as a newcomer to the US. She was becoming self-aware and politically aware at the same time.

Mom was a light-skinned Mexican woman with privilege and style. For all intents and purposes, she might have passed for white except for her extraordinarily thick accent and her unmistakable Latina looks. But because of her Black and Jewish and feminist friends, she was learning words like "discrimination" and "racism" and "feminism." Her Jewish girlfriends told her that it was okay for people to live together without getting married, which would have been scandalous in Mexico. Mom's Black friend Rosa told her about all the places she couldn't go in Chicago because of segregation. Regular places like restaurants and hotels and shops would not admit her as a paying customer just because of her skin color.

The stories they shared rang true to Mom. Now she could put into words some of the things she had witnessed herself: the way people treated our family when we left Hyde Park, the visible and entrenched poverty in Pilsen, the all-Black neighborhoods of the South Side. The people who put up with this kind of discrimination were also our neighbors and friends. It was confusing.

Bertha Elena, who was fifteen, had already been attending protests for months. My sister had been secretly ditching class to help organize demonstrations with the Student Mobilization Committee, the Black Student Union, and the Young Socialist Alliance at Kenwood Academy High School, which was a hotbed for activism. Not long before this, one of her classmates, a Black student, was shot and killed on campus by a white police officer. This event mobilized the school and greater community like no other. My sister was one of the activists who helped coordinate the response by organizing sit-ins, boycotts, and massive parent meetings. Students and parents demanded that the school provide higher quality education to Black students, offer more courses on Black history, and make other general improvements. Through all of these efforts, they ended up shutting down the entire high school for a full day. It was an act of protest that ended with the police arresting twenty-two students. One of their unmet demands was to name a room in the school for Fred Hampton, the Black Panther murdered by the FBI. The event changed my sister forever because it connected her to her community but also to protest movements all over the world.

Bertha Elena had been influenced years before, but I just didn't catch the clues. She understood why our grammar school teacher Ms. Rawls wore all black every day, including black shoes, knee-high boots, stockings, and black eyeliner outlining her already deep and dark eyes. She wore a black beret, so it should have been obvious that she was a supporter of the Black Panthers. The Black Panthers had a philosophy about how to understand what was happening in the world and, when Bertha was in Mrs. Rawls's eighth-grade class, we heard about it during our family dinners.

The war between the US and Vietnam wasn't just going on in a faraway country. The battle over whether or not the US should even be fighting in Vietnam was happening steps away from where I lived. If I felt this way as an eight-year-old, it was even more real for my teenage sister. She had friends whose older brothers had their numbers called for the draft. Young men who were not that much older than her were being put on planes and sent over to Vietnam to fight in this war. Many would not return. She also knew conscientious objectors, or COs, who refused to fight and left for Canada to get away.

Attending the protest with my mom and brothers and sister marked my birth as a politically conscious human being, at eight years old. And I will never stop thanking my mother for writing that note to Mrs. Jaye and giving me a chance to watch my teacher scoff at me. Sure, I was scared, but I would survive that—and so much more.

CHAPTER 7

Putting Down Roots

While mom was getting into the flow of American life, it felt like Dad was holding back. Was he in or was he out? Sometimes it seemed that his frustration played out in, well, some silly ways.

Papi hated pets in general and indoor animals in specific. I mean, *hated* them. My father had grown up on a ranch and was forced to tend to the cattle and horses. He could never understand how anybody could have a dog living inside with them, much less a cat. But we were city kids and all the kids around us had pets. We wanted that American thing too. Since there were four of us and we were pretty demanding, somehow or other, a couple of pets made their way into our house.

Our first pet was a light blue parakeet named Benny who had an extraordinarily adorable personality. Dad wasn't much interested in him at first, but he had agreed to take the bird as a favor for a colleague who was moving and couldn't take

Benny with him. Papi didn't know how to say no. In the beginning, Benny stayed locked in his cage even though his previous owner had left his cage open all the time.

I've come to believe that birds have individual personalities and carry profound wisdom. We watched Dad slowly become enchanted by Benny. Soon he was allowed to live outside his cage and was free to fly around the apartment. His favorite thing to do was to perch near the stove and pick the salt off the tortillas my mother cooked in a frying pan every morning. The other thing Benny loved to do was to fly over to my father and sit on his shoulder. Occasionally, he would land smack dab on the bald head of my father, who, surprisingly, loved it. He was delighted that this bird loved him so much. It was a hint that my stern Mexican dad was actually a softie.

That was how it started. Soon we adopted a cat named Nagoose. Don't ask me where that name came from, but Nagoose was a great family cat. She loved to be hugged and carried around the house, though not by my father. Unlike with Benny, dad never took to the cat.

Nagoose, as the saying goes, definitely had nine lives. She loved to sit by the windows and watch the goings-on in the street below. One warm summer day in Chicago, Nagoose sat on the window ledge and leaned against the screen that was up to keep the mosquitoes out. The heat made her drowsy and she fell asleep with all her weight pushing against it. All of a sudden the screen popped out and Nagoose was awakened as she fell out the window. Somehow, as she whipped through the air past the three floors, she righted herself and landed on her feet.

This made all of us kids love her more, but dad was just angry.

Since Nagoose was already a year old when we got her, she had to be "fixed." That's what they called it when you neutered a cat. It's a procedure to remove their reproductive organs so they can't have babies. So off she went to surgery.

When Nagoose came home, she had a long line of stitches along her belly. She didn't like the stitches, the itching, or the pain. So she picked at her stitches until they came open. My mother had to grab the cat and hold her to make sure her intestines didn't fall out all over the place. Luckily, Nagoose survived, but there went another of her lives. The stitches incident, though, was the last straw for my dad, and not long after that, Nagoose, with seven lives left to go, was given away. I intensely disliked my father at this precise moment, but I didn't know what to do with all my emotions.

Nagoose the cat and Benny the parakeet were memorable parts of the years my family lived in our first Chicago apartment. We had an indoor patio at the front of the apartment where mom and I would watch TV and do our midday exercises. There was a small living room, my mom and dad's bedroom, and a bathroom next to that. My sister and I shared a small bedroom with two beds. Then there was a small dining room area, my brothers' bedroom off to the side, the kitchen in the back, and one more small bedroom with a bathroom.

It sounds huge with all those rooms, but everything was closely packed together—and we liked it that way. Uno encima del otro, one on top of the other, which is so Mexican and I love that! Because the apartment was smaller, it felt warmer and, in some way, more connected to Mexico.

In those early years we weren't able to travel back to Mexico for the holidays, so we celebrated Christmas in Chicago by incorporating some of our Mexican traditions in a small and private way. Every year for Christmas, my mom would build an extensive nacimiento, or "the birthing" in Spanish, which is a nativity scene to depict the birth of Jesus Christ.

My mom spent hours creating intricate nacimientos to display on a built-in wooden and glass vanity in our dining room. Nobody else in our neighborhood had little baby Jesuses, fake ponds made of foil, and miniature trees with cotton tips to make them look like they'd just been dusted with fresh snow. This annual ritual always felt like a secret thing our family did together in that apartment.

One day late in 1969, Mom and Dad went out on their own and I was left behind with my brothers and sister. They rarely went out together like that unless they were going shopping for us kids. Something was up. Then I began to hear words like "apartment" and "condominium" being spoken around the house in Spanish. I didn't understand what it all meant until my parents revealed that they had decided to buy an apartment. They wanted to own something in the US instead of renting.

This wasn't just a big purchase; it was also an act of putting down roots. Owning a house or apartment had an air of permanency to it. My mom had convinced my dad to move to the United States, and now she was convincing him to buy property.

The first time I saw the new apartment was the day we moved in the spring of 1970. Everything about the place felt huge. With more than three thousand square feet, it had five bedrooms, plus a living room, dining room, and eat-in kitchen. Unlike our old apartment, where the stairs to the back door were exposed to the elements, the stairs to the back door in the new apartment, which led straight to my room, were in a covered stairwell so you could stay nice and warm.

There were totally different smells in this building. Our old neighbors over on Cornell Street had been Jewish Australian psychotherapists, an orthodox Jewish family, and a young Polish couple. I had learned lessons just by going up the three flights, and now I would learn new ones. Our new neighbors on the first floor were the Hans. The kids spoke perfect English, but their mom and dad didn't. They cooked traditional Chinese food all the time. On the second floor there was a Jewish family who kept kosher, and on the third floor was us, the Spanish-speaking Mexican family.

Our apartment had an extended hallway. It was so long it felt like the length of a city block. Of course, my brothers and I saw it as our personal speedway and daily raced each other down the hallway to the back rooms where we slept overlooking a typical Chicago alley. Several times a day for the rest of our lives, it seemed, my father would tell us to stop running.

The best part was that I finally had my own room in the back. But that was also a little scary. I liked sharing a bedroom with my sister. It had given me access to everything about her—her style, her makeup, her music, her brain. Now she had a room of her own with her own bathroom that Mom and Dad had decided to redo in a black and white mod style with a shag rug. Her bedroom also had a lot of mirrors, which was very 1970s. Truly a great era in American home decor if you like bling.

My room, on the other hand, was done up in a pastel floral theme in pink and peach wallpaper. It didn't bother me, but I didn't love it either. There were a lot of flowers for four walls. But at least it was all my own. I had the same furniture that had been in my old bedroom, because we couldn't afford anything new. For a long time, I was ashamed of the old wooden furniture in my bedroom because my wealthier Jewish girlfriends had top-of-the-line bedroom sets. That was not going to happen for me, at least not for a while. I would receive a new chest of drawers when I was thirteen as an eighth-grade graduation gift.

I also had a porch off the back of my room next to the staircase that overlooked the alley, but it was falling apart when we bought the apartment, so we could never go out on it. Sometimes, on my own, I would open the creaky aluminum back door to the porch. On the other side of the alley was a single room occupancy (SRO) building, which is a kind of housing built for people with low incomes. The rooms are small and tenants usually have to share communal kitchens and bathrooms. The place looked so different from our apartment and yet it was just across the alley. Many of the people who lived in the SROs were disabled or mentally challenged.

I was often frightened by the things I heard and saw from

the back door. It was like a portal to a secret and mysterious side of Hyde Park. One night I saw a woman standing outside in her nightgown and a man yelling at her. Another night I heard a kid crying loudly for hours and no one seemed to care. I didn't tell anyone what I saw or heard, but I spent a lot of time with the door open, thinking about the lives on the other side of the alley. I listened to the sounds of loneliness and sadness as well as wild parties.

Even though my family could now afford to live in this nice apartment, it came with a lot of sacrifice. My parents' official line was, *We have enough money to buy this nice home, but don't ask for anything else because it's not in the budget. No new clothes, no new shoes, no nothing.* We were going to be on an austerity program for what felt like forever. There was never money for anything extra or nice-to-have—just the basics.

The other key feature of our new, palatial apartment, and the thing that sold my dad on it, was a bedroom that was converted into a library with bookshelves on all four walls. My dad now had a study of his own, and that was partly why he agreed to buy an apartment in a city and a country that he was not yet completely committed to or comfortable living in. The only things he was 100 percent committed to were his family and the electron microscope. But this room was important to my father. It was almost as if having a library of his own signified his intelligence and affirmed his genius in the United States of America.

A couple of shelves were devoted to Spanish-language books from Mexico. A few were filled with family photo albums. Then there was a long shelf with my father's *National Geographic* collection that he had started back in Mexico. Each magazine was put in perfect order by date. As kids, we were always encouraged to pull out a *National Geographic* and browse its pages as long as we put it right back where we got it from. My family also purchased a set of World Book Encyclopedias, a sort of status symbol of moving up in the world, and that took up another couple of shelves. Then there were my father's medical books that I learned never to look at because they had photographs of diseases like the mumps, and broken bones, which terrified me.

The previous owners were from Iran and had recently renovated the apartment. Apparently, they were very wealthy, and had a sense of style that we found over the top. Part of the deal when my parents bought the apartment was that they agreed not to immediately paint over any of the wallpaper. One of the prints was based on a famous tapestry on display in some museum and the outgoing owners couldn't bear to see it ripped out. The wallpaper pattern in the dining room, supposedly, was a reproduction of Egyptian hieroglyphs. The living room wallpaper was flecked with gold, while the kitchen had the craziest pattern that looked like a massive explosion of flowers. All the bright colors were dizzying. People who came over to visit said the walls gave them a headache just looking at them.

Although I didn't really understand our family's finances, I knew that buying a home was a big deal that took a lot of effort. I was really proud of my parents for being able to do that. It also signaled to me that I didn't have to worry that we might one day up and leave Chicago. Every time we went to Mexico, my parents were faced with the nagging suspicion that maybe they should be raising their kids there instead of the US. *Isn't it better for them to be with their family? Look at all the culture we're missing out on. Now that we can see and appreciate Mexico from a distance, shouldn't we be giving this to our kids?*

The purchase of our new home made it pretty clear to me: We weren't moving back to Mexico any time soon and we weren't moving anywhere else either. Our family was putting down roots in a permanent way that felt great. This apartment, Mom and Dad owned it. It was ours. That also meant Hyde Park was mine. Chicago was mine. My life was grounded here, where Lorraine and Mrs. Turner, Emmett and Elizabeth, Susie and Derek, Pilsen and Bret Harte Elementary, and all my friends, teachers, and neighbors were. I was exactly where I was supposed to be—in Chicago—and that felt right, even though our hearts were often someplace else.

CHAPTER 8

A Different Kind of Church

Before we moved to the new apartment, we had one television set. It was a huge, black-and-white TV in a clunky wooden frame that sat in the living room. Having a television at all was a big deal because it meant your family had some sort of disposable income. Televisions were a luxury item. Not everyone had one. But if you wanted to know what was going on in pop culture and the world, being able to tune in to the latest program was essential.

Since there was only one television set, my dad basically set the tone for what could be watched and when. We usually watched programs together. On one occasion, the entire family sat down to watch *The Flying Nun*. Yes, there was a show called *The Flying Nun* and it starred a young Sally Field. The habit she wore on her head gave her the magical power of flight. A funny Catholic nun! (Maybe that says it all about the late 1960s.)

Some of the other shows I liked to watch when I was

around eight years old were *The Addams Family*, *The Andy Griffith Show*, and *The Dick Van Dyke Show*. One night we gathered around the TV while we ate dinner and watched Ed Sullivan interview the Beatles on his show. I fell in love with Ringo because he was the most geeky and the least popular of the four band members. My dad was not pleased, by the way. The whole concept of having crushes on boys was for American girls, and in his opinion, I was not one of them.

Moments like that made me feel like I was hip to what was happening in this country. Television brought people together. TV programs, especially the most popular ones, were like events that everyone wanted to attend. Even if you didn't have a television set, you found somebody who did. You had to have patience because most programs were on only once a week. You spent the entire week looking forward to watching the next episode of your favorite TV show, and you made sure to watch at the right time. There was no way to stop it and rewind if something happened and you missed it. That was it. The next day after a big program had aired, people would talk about what they had watched and it made you feel closer to one another, like you had something in common, even if it was just witnessing a specific moment. Watching the Beatles on Ed Sullivan was one of those moments.

The TV shows were about people, usually white men, who were doing all kinds of interesting things. I guess we were supposed to want to become like them because they were the only role models I saw on television. I didn't have a way to understand this at the time, but I knew in my gut that I was an outsider in the US because people like me and my family, Mexicans and Latinos and immigrants, were never portrayed on that box. TV dramas and funny sitcoms were for white men, their coworkers, and their families.

Around the same time, I stopped speaking Spanish at home. My parents continued to address me and my siblings only in Spanish, but we answered them in English. They were not happy about this development and tried to get us to stick to our Spanish. There was no chance, though. It was four kids against two adults, so the kids won.

Despite the TV's Americanizing influence, after we moved into the new apartment, my dad relented and allowed my mother to buy another, smaller television for the kitchen and dining room area where she spent a lot of her day doing housework like cooking and folding clothes. This way she could be entertained while doing so. My parents did a lot of research on television models trying to find the best deal and decided on a Sony Trinitron color TV for the kitchen. The big, hulking black-and-white TV moved into my parents' bedroom. Once that happened, the new color TV was on all the time and us kids got a little more say over which shows the dial was turned to (back then there were only a few channels and TVs had big knobs that you turned manually to change the channel). This was before the days of cable television, so there was no such thing as twenty-four-hour programming and most channels went off the air during the night and sometimes for parts of the day.

Mom usually arrived home from her volunteer work in the afternoon and at four o'clock she'd start watching the local news. I'd watch as I sat nearby doing my homework. I came to understand the difference between the local news and the national news. The local news was about my new city, Chicago, and the national news was about my new country. But I knew this country was only partially mine. I lived here but I wasn't a citizen, a fact that was never far from my mind.

The people who delivered the news on the national networks were all men. Their names were Walter Cronkite, Harry Reasoner, Garrick Utley, John Chancellor. All white men, too. Journalists and the news media were revered in our household like A-list celebrities. My parents put tremendous value on following the news and staying informed, and on the role of television news in particular. I think it had to do with the fact that English was not Mom and Dad's native language and they didn't grow up reading in English. Watching and listening to TV anchors deliver the news live worked for them in a way that newspapers didn't.

Besides, what we were living through was so visually engulfing. We saw plenty of video footage of the Vietnam War itself and of the massive anti-war protests, sometimes joyous, sometimes angry, in big cities like Chicago, New York, and Washington, D.C. There were marches for civil rights, like the one I attended, and women's protests where women demanded to be seen and heard, to have their work and bodies respected and protected by the laws of this country. It was extraordinary, but it wasn't the first time that American women had stood up together. The collective action of the suffragettes at the beginning of the twentieth century had paved the path for women to secure the right to vote in 1920 with the passing of the Nineteenth Amendment—white women, that is.

The late 1960s and early '70s were also an era of shifting cultural values. Many people, especially teenagers and young adults, were questioning authority and the morals of their parents' generation. Society became more open-minded and accepting of experimentation in all sorts of fields and areas of life. Hundreds of thousands of young people flocked to Bethel, a quiet town in upstate New York, for an epic music festival called Woodstock that promised "3 Days of Peace and Music." People attended wearing tie-dye and fringe. All of this was being captured on the news, too.

I wanted to be in that television set, to be at those places shown on the news. I wanted to see it for myself. Though I never said it out loud, I thought those men who got to work as journalists had cool jobs. There were almost zero female journalists on TV then. Can you imagine not ever seeing a female journalist? It sent a message to me as a girl that maybe women just couldn't do that kind of job.

Sundays soon became the most important day for television in our house. In the beginning, we went to church on Sundays, but that didn't last long because my dad was a scientist and my mom didn't believe that intensely. After I received my First Communion when I was seven years old, a major rite of passage in the Catholic religion, we basically stopped going to church. Instead, watching *CBS Sunday Morning* and *60 Minutes* became our Sunday visit to a church of a different kind.

Funnily enough, *CBS Sunday Morning* usually came on

right after a televised sermon. Charles Kuralt was the program's first anchor, and he would take viewers across the United States of America with his incredible reporting. As a young girl, I hadn't seen much of the rest of the country yet, and this helped me see and learn about it. The program's human-oriented storytelling made me feel included because it revealed that there were all kinds of quirky people making their lives in this country, different but the same, just like in Hyde Park.

On Sunday nights, the typical family meal of breaded chicken breasts, macaroni and cheese, and green beans with either chipotles or jalapeños en escabeche, was accompanied by more journalism. We sat around the table eating dinner while we watched *60 Minutes*. During this weekly ritual, nobody spoke or interrupted so we could hear every single word of the report being broadcast. *60 Minutes* earned a reputation for doing fearless investigative journalism that asked hard questions of important people and demanded answers. The program was respected because it aspired to hold the government and those with power accountable to the people.

The journalists on *60 Minutes* were brave and spoke up for the people. When someone they wanted to speak to refused to give them an interview, they found other ways to get to them. They would stop leaders in the middle of the street or catch them walking out of their home and press them with questions, or read back terrible things they might have said. *60 Minutes* inspired me. I was beginning to understand that journalism, in the form of a free and independent press, was another important pillar of democratic expression.

You know that saying, "Knowledge is power"? What I learned from watching TV helped me realize I could take action in response to the issues I believed were important. The TV told us about Cesar Chavez and Dolores Huerta, the Mexican American labor activists who were organizing grape workers in California to strike against low wages and poor working conditions. They asked people to boycott grapes until the workers' demands were met by their employers. Soon our family stopped buying grapes in solidarity with these farm workers.

The environmental movement was beginning to raise awareness about pollution and endangered species. People used to throw garbage on the street all the time. There was a garbage heap next to an abandoned building only fifty steps away from our house. Environmentalists spoke about the need for everyone to help reduce waste and keep our planet healthy. Soon I was writing letters in support of environmental issues, about protecting endangered wolves and whales, and we did a garbage cleanup in our alley.

I didn't know then that both *CBS Sunday Morning* and *60 Minutes*, the two shows my family watched religiously every Sunday, would end up being pillars in my life as a journalist. I never could have imagined that I would one day model my own work after these journalists. You never know when something you do as a kid, because it's fun or you find it interesting, will plant the seed for what you're going to do when you grow up. Even though I didn't see anyone like me doing the work of a journalist, something in me fell in love with it and planted a seed that eventually blossomed. It was a damn strong seed!

CHAPTER 9

The Drive South

The TV wasn't just about the news. We were learning about American culture. On *The Brady Bunch*, having single parents was normalized. We were seeing more women who were working outside of the home. I also learned this from watching television: Every. Single. Family. FIGHTS.

In our family there were a few predictable triggers that would always set off an argument. Most of them had to do with my mom's increasing desire to work outside the home. Everybody recognized that she worked hard at home doing washing and cleaning and cooking and making sure the household ran smoothly. In Mexico, we say women drive their homes—manejan su casa bien—so a house is like a car. Now that I was eight years old, going on nine, I could walk to school with my brothers and sister. I wasn't even coming home for lunch every day because I had friends at school now. Mom wanted to do more than just stay in the house all day; she wanted a job outside it. As far as my father was concerned, that was not the bargain he had made when they got married according to traditional male and female roles and values back in Mexico. There were lots of conversations with raised voices about Mom wanting to get a job. Eventually, my parents decided to go to couples therapy together to work through these disagreements.

There were also fights about the clothes my sister wore. It was the 1970s and miniskirts were all the rage. Wearing your hair with a deep side part so that half your hair would cascade down over one of your eyes was the highest of high fashion. Both things annoyed and angered my dad. He also did not want my sister, who was now fifteen years old, to have absolutely anything to do with boys. Of course, that didn't stop her. This was the same sister who was already ditching high school to organize and attend protest rallies.

I didn't understand why my dad was so tightly wound about the women in our family, but I was beginning to see that Papi held rigid views on issues of gender. Why did they have to fight about how my sister dressed and whether she could have a boyfriend? Why didn't my dad simply trust my sister, the way he did my brothers? Girls and boys were not treated equally in Mexican households. From my dad's perspective, a daughter is supposed to do what her father tells her. Answering back was too American for him.

There was one surefire trigger that always started a family fight no matter what. It happened once a year, right on time, at the start of our annual trip to Mexico. My dad would drive all six of us to Mexico City, and the big fight was always around how much luggage we could fit in the long, green station wagon, which Papi protected as if it was a newborn baby.

Our Mexican family was full of consumers who wanted the latest American products, which put pressure on our family to transport their requested purchases across the border, and in turn led to these explosive fights. From Dad's point of view, it was like, *How dare you risk damaging my prized possession by filling it up with such ridiculous things?* Meanwhile, Mom was hell-bent on packing as much stuff as possible into the car, including contraband, as if it were a jigsaw puzzle. By contraband, I mean a computer or a blender. It was illegal for Mexicans to buy American-made things without paying sky-high taxes. My mom would stuff a computer in a pillowcase and then we would pretend to sleep on it as we crossed the border into Mexico.

Exasperated, my dad would threaten, "Pues, no voy. I'm not going to Mexico. Unload the car, take everything back upstairs to the third floor. I am not going. If you insist on taking that last suitcase, which could very well cause the muffler to scrape the bumpy roads in Mexico and damage the car, then we cannot do it. Bertha, you are pushing it. Ya no tengo paciencia para esto! No soporto mas, cargar todo esto para todo el mundo. I'm sick of being the transport animal, the donkey, the burro for all our family members who want these things. They don't need them!"

Around this point, Mom would tell us all to go sit in the car and act as if we were going to leave soon. I usually cried. The thing is, we knew that we were going to Mexico. In fact, my father was the person who most wanted to go to Mexico, and he was also the person in the family who loved driving the most. The trip covered more than two thousand miles. He got to drive eight hours a day and steer his family through the US to the motherland. He was our guide, our protector, the leader of the pack, which was the role he loved to play. But he also loved his car very much. Anything that put his car in danger was always a source of tension.

We inevitably got on the road and within ninety minutes, as soon as we got outside the city, I was asking for the plastic bag to throw up into. That's when I learned what "psychosomatic" means. It's when a physical illness is caused not by outside factors like a virus or an accident, but by the mind itself due to stress or anxiety. My family told me I was psychosomatic because it was my brain telling my body to throw up, which I did once or twice and then I'd be fine. It was just what I needed to do to relieve the stress of our family fighting and then leaving on this big annual road trip. My entire family laughed and jeered at me, except for my mother who would hold my head over the plastic bag as I vomited. I really did feel sick, though, and I did not appreciate being laughed at. I didn't know this word for it at the time, but I was managing my anxiety on my own.

By the time my puking was taken care of, we were usually in southern Illinois and then making our way through St. Louis, Missouri, the next big city on our route. I'd look out the window and stare at the massive Gateway Arch as we drove past. In many ways, I was incredibly lucky to have this experience of traveling by car through the heartland of the United States of America.

We stopped at diners and gas stations along the highway for meals and fill-ups. At the end of a long day on the road we'd pull into a Holiday Inn or maybe a Best Western. If we were lucky, they'd have a color TV and a swimming pool. We wouldn't have time to go swimming, and besides, it was December. But we thought having a pool nearby made us cool.

My parents would go into the motel office to check in and would usually tell the person at the front desk that there were only two of us kids, because motels charged by the person. The two unaccounted for, which always included me, would have to slink down in the back of the car and hide to not be seen. Once the coast was clear, we'd pile into our rooms. Sometimes we'd get two rooms that were connected or adjacent to each other. Other times, if money was really tight, we would all be crammed together into one room with cots.

One thing our parents were adamant about was showing respect for the different kinds of people we saw and interacted with on these trips. Chicago was the second largest city in the United States, after New York and ahead of Los Angeles, and as city kids, the four of us thought we were more sophisticated than everybody else.

Traveling down the center of the US, most of the people we encountered were white and spoke with thick Southern accents. We all had a hard time understanding them, but us kids could eventually figure out what they were saying. They sometimes had trouble understanding our parents, as well. We would often have to translate for my mom and dad, like the time we stopped at a toll booth to pay the toll and my dad asked the lady in the booth if she knew where the nearest gas station was.

"Can you tell me, please, where is the nearest gas station?" Dad asked. But the way he said it sounded more like, "Coood chu pleeze tell miiii querrr eees da neeeeeerest gases estatione?"

The lady kept saying in a Southern drawl, "Excuse me, what?" over and over again. In this particular instance, she couldn't understand my father because of *his* accent. After a while one of us yelled from the back, "Where's the nearest gas station?" And then we laughed about it and maybe made my dad feel bad about his very thick Mexican accent.

One time in Texarkana we got breakfast first thing in the morning at the motel diner. The waitress who seated us spoke with a pronounced Southern accent. When she came to take our order, all of us kids, except for my sister, placed our orders by imitating her accent. My father had been laughed at for so long because of his accent, so I thought somehow that it was appropriate to do that to someone else. Mom and Dad did not agree. As soon as we finished our breakfast, our very angry mother told us to stand outside.

"What?" my brothers and I asked in shock.

"Put your coats and gloves on, and go stand outside. You stay out there until we're done eating. You don't treat people like that. You don't make fun of people because of the way they speak. We will not tolerate it."

That taught me a lesson I never forgot. Our parents would not let us make fun of the white people we encountered. They knew that we, as immigrants, had been made fun of for too long, that Black people and other people of color had been made fun of for too long. But we were not going to be a part of that cycle of tearing people down just because they were different from us. They were not going to allow that to happen. The different ways that people talk throughout the US now fascinate me.

As we drove on, we continued to pass through towns most people in Chicago had never heard of. Outside of Chicago, we seemed to see Black people only behind the scenes—working in service roles as elevator operators and doormen. And in Texas, the few people who looked like or sounded like us we usually saw working in the kitchen. This left me with a lot of unanswered questions. Why did Black and Brown people seem to disappear in these other states? Where were the Black and Brown people here who didn't work in service jobs? How did the massive highways connecting North to South fail to capture these faces and places?

Out of all the regions we drove through, Texas was the toughest because it was the longest, flattest, straightest state. At least in Mexico, every now and then you'd see some road-kill. But not on Texas roads. There weren't a lot of billboards either, so we couldn't even play the alphabet game where we'd piece together the alphabet by calling out the words we saw on billboards and license plates. It was just nothing for miles. We got so bored.

That's when my brother would start dropping fart bombs. The rest of us kids would alert everyone by making the sound of a siren going "woo, woo, woo." Since we always made these trips during December for the holidays, it was freezing outside and too cold to roll down the windows. We had no choice but to deal with these stinky assaults on our noses, so we did so with humor. We were not so much a burping family (although my sister was queen of the burps) as we were a farting one. This entertained my father to no end. That's right: The serious scientist who loved to spend his time nerding out on molecules would fall into uncontrollable laughter about anything that had to do with farts. Flatulence became our entertainment for the flat roads of Texas.

The crossover into Mexico was easy. We were never searched or tagged or targeted like we were by US immigration agents. Us kids would scream with joy and applaud when we drove by the old toll booth–size immigration checkpoint that represented the official entry into Mexico. Here the immigration officials would just wave every single car through. I loved that we were being welcomed into a country that trusted us.

Once we crossed into Mexico, all the radio stations changed and I'd begin to feel a little alienated. I was excited about going south into Mexico, but I also knew that other things came along with it. My cousins would tease and bully me about being an American girl. On the flip side, there would be an endless number of hugs and smooches from grandparents, aunts and uncles, and cousins. I started to imagine the smells and flavors of all my favorite Mexican dishes.

Still, there was also a feeling of unpredictability that came with diving into a world that was like a kaleidoscope of colors, people, and new experiences, wobbly and not clean-cut like the more predictable USA. I was overwhelmed with excitement, yet hearing Spanish-language radio would suddenly make me long for the R&B stations we were leaving behind. The fact that I felt that way worried me. Why did I yearn for American pop culture? Did that mean I was a vendida, a sellout?

Once, as we were driving through the northern part of Mexico near Chihuahua, we were stopped on an empty road by a group of men carrying machine guns. They looked like soldiers, but not exactly. My dad told us, in a voice that sounded worried, not to say a word and to remain calm. He rolled down the window and when he opened his mouth he spoke in a stern tone I had never heard before. He sounded like a gorilla protecting his family.

The leader of the group asked us to open the glove compartment and my father did as he said. There was nothing in it and they could see we had nothing to give them. Then my father said, "It's time for us to move on." He didn't even offer what we all knew was hidden in our car—cash for a mordida, a bribe. He would not respond to what he saw as thuggery. Of course we were scared, but in this case we were lucky to drive away unscathed.

We were wary of the police in general, especially those in Mexico City. They were to be feared and a hassle to be avoided. On many occasions, they would see our family driving around in an American car with a license plate that said Illinois and pull us over. *It's Christmas, sir. Algo para mi familia? Algo para la Navidad?* they would say, hinting that they would disappear for a few bucks. My father would be humiliated into bribing them. This happened a lot. Papi hated the corruption in his beloved Madre Patria.

When we finally arrived in Mexico City, we piled into Tia Lila's small, Mexican-size three-bedroom, two-story casita on la Calle Pitagoras in la Colonia Navarte with the rest of our extended family, which felt like squeezing into a hotel room with fifty people. Because I was one of the youngest and tiniest, I got assigned to sleep on the little foot sofa next to the windows. Did I mention there was no central heating in Mexico City apartments and homes? Thankfully, I had about ten San Marcos blankets thrown on me. My grandmother and one of my cousins slept in the same room as me, while my parents and my sister and brothers slept in another room. The rest of the boy cousins slept downstairs on sofas. There were bodies everywhere.

We always woke up to the smell of tortillas and eggs being fried for the first round of huevos con tortillas abajo, perfectly cooked sunny-side-up eggs on a lightly fried and salted tortilla, served with ketchup for the American kids and homemade salsa for our older cousins. We spent most of our days playing on the streets, visiting family, and eating a lot.

Our mission every visit was to find the best street tacos in Mexico City. We would travel across the city to try places out (literally pulling up to a corner intersection), but in the end, we decided that the best tacos were at a taqueria only a stone's throw away from Echegaray in the new so-called colonia known as Satelite, literally a suburban satellite of Mexico City.

My family had left Mexico City to try and live the suburban American life, which had been frowned on because everybody in Mexico hated the United States. Yet, as I was observing for myself, everybody in Mexico also wanted to be like the United States. My Tía Gloria, another one of my mom's sisters, had just left la Narvarte in the city to move to this American-style suburban retreat.

It turned out this taqueria had moved from downtown Mexico City to the suburbs around the edges just like my family had. They made carne asada with cebollas asadas, palm-size corn tortillas for the tacos, and queso fundido like nothing you've seen before, in small homemade clay cazuelas dripping all over and served with warm homemade flour tortillas. More than a dozen of us, my siblings and primos and I, showed up at the taqueria and ordered dozens upon dozens of tacos. Each taco came with a little paper slip on your plate, and at the end of the meal they'd count up the papelitos to calculate the bill.

My mother, like me, was the baby of her family, and my grandfather loved his baby girl. Our family visits to Mexico were one of the few times of the year that he would slow down and take a break from managing his trucking and crane company, which was named after him. Abuelito would take us to wild places. On almost every trip, we'd go downtown to Restaurante Miramar and my grandfather would treat my father to his favorite dish, Vuelve a La Vida, which is a huge mixed seafood cocktail served in a glass, kind of like a shrimp cocktail but Mexican style with fresh salsa at the bottom. The rest of us ate endless peeled shrimp, something that our family could definitely not afford in the United States.

One time my grandfather took us to a Yucatec restaurant, since his roots were from the Yucatan. Another time he took us to a restaurant that served traditional Mexican food based on recipes that dated back hundreds of years. These dishes were kept alive through the centuries by Mexico's Indigenous peoples. They also served tacos with gusanos (caterpillars) and chapulines (grasshoppers). I did not eat those because I thought it was gross then, but nowadays I'll try almost anything when it comes to food. (The grasshoppers are crunchy and salty like popcorn, though I don't know if I'd eat them during a movie!)

My parents made a point of taking us to see specific sites while we were in Mexico. We always made a trip to the Museo Nacional de Antropología, the museum with the world's largest collection of ancient Mexican art, and a visit to Teotihuacán, an ancient city that was once the center of Aztec life. There, we would climb the pyramids of the sun and moon. The experience left us with a deep appreciation for the power of nature. We learned about Tlaloc, the rain god, and Quetzalcoatl, the god of all gods, symbolized by a massive eagle clutching a serpent in its beak and claws.

We saw the power and beauty of these ancient cultures but also their link to the present day through the Indigenous people who continue to carry on their traditions. Our parents instilled us with respect for our Indigenous roots by taking us to places where we could see the origins of the culture for ourselves. Without having to say so, our parents were teaching us where we came from, and to love and respect it. These types of explorations became an essential part of my travels in Mexico.

Going to archeological sites in Palenque that were farther outside Mexico City and deep in the jungle was like getting a shot of ancestral adrenaline. My Mexican cousins bullied me for being too American or for loving my Indigenous side too much, while my classmates back in Chicago bullied me because I was Mexican-born and had a green card. Yep, you get twice as much bullying when you are bicultural! Knowing where I came from and seeing the beauty and power of my culture gave me the strength to deal with the bullying I was receiving on both ends.

My parents never stopped in their quest to have us visit as many archeological sites as we could every time we visited Mexico. I was that lucky kid who got to see the Olmec heads in Villahermosa and the tombs of Mayan kings in Chichen Itza that are blocked off today and no one can get to them anymore. We would fight our claustrophobia and explore the tiny stone passageways deep in the innards of the pyramids, drenched with sweat, to find centuries-old statues and sculptures and offerings left in the tombs. My father would take out his camera and snap a picture of the Maya king's resting place buried inside Palenque's central pyramid, El Templo de las Inscripciones.

Most of the sites didn't even have a parking lot for visitors back then. That's how rundown and untended to they were, which tells you how little the Mexican government cared about Indigenous history and civilization. But us kids took advantage of this and ran up and down the pyramids like they were jungle gyms. No one stopped us. We would sit and lay our heads on the bodies of the chacmool statues, where the Mayans would place the hearts of the young women and men they sacrificed to the gods. We thought it was funny to pretend we had been sacrificed too.

We were also learning that here in Mexico, just like in the United States, you do not make fun of people for what they look like, how they talk, what they're wearing, or how they've been conditioned in life. At every gas station, my mother would open the back door of our station wagon and pass out clothes from a large suitcase filled with hand-me-downs to the boys who worked at the gas station wiping windshields.

We spoke to anyone and everyone. People who treated our family with respect were treated with respect in return. If you treated us differently because we had American license plates or because we spoke Spanish with a heavy American accent, my mom wasn't having it. For her, it was all about treating people equally.

I never saw any family fights within our family of six or among our larger family of grandparents, aunts, uncles, and cousins during our stays in Mexico. Everybody was so happy to have us back. (Later on, I came to realize arguments did happen but often after the kids were asleep.)

Our family was the only one out of the entire extended family on both sides that had left. We were extraterrestrials because my mother and father were living outside the norm in a place that was very different, very cold, and very far away. We were treated like foreign specimens, but also with love and admiration. We were bullied, but we were also hugged. They insulted my dad for being an American citizen, but they also moved closer to my father to feel some of his shine. They wanted a little piece of it because everybody knew he was a bit of a genius. Now that genius had led him to Chicago or, as they called it back then, Cheee-cah-goooooh.

Our trips to Mexico, which had us crossing real, visible borders, also grounded and rooted us in the world. They made me realize that the world was so much more than Chicago, so much more than the United States. The world was bigger and more complicated than I could ever imagine. My parents had made the decision to share that world with us, even as they themselves were still finding their way in it. We were strangers in a new country and sometimes we were treated like strangers in our own land. Together, the six of us were going to figure this all out.

CHAPTER 10

A Girl Named Maria

When my sister was seventeen and I was ten, she got invited to a watch party for the movie *West Side Story* with all her friends from Kenwood High School.

The musical *West Side Story* first opened on Broadway in 1957, with music written by Leonard Bernstein. It was a huge hit and ran for nearly two years. The play is essentially a modern-day interpretation of *Romeo and Juliet*, which is the story of a young woman and man from two very different backgrounds who fall in love and want to be together, but can't because their families are enemies.

The film premiered in movie theaters in 1961. A decade later it came to the small screen to make its television debut that spring of 1972. This was a very big deal. Me and my friends had all heard of the movie, but we'd never had the chance to see it. This was before the invention of DVDs or even VHS tapes made it easy to rewatch classic films at home. So it was a rare event when Hollywood movies got aired on prime-time television and was something not to be missed. Everyone in the entire school would be watching—and then talking about it the next week in class. And if you were a teenager, you had to see it because it was a story about teenage love and there would be full body contact and kisses and that was very unusual for TV.

But my father didn't want Bertha Elena to go to the watch party.

Despite being the only one in his family to buck convention by moving to the United States, my dad was a traditional Mexican father. He had been raised by a father who grew up in the deep-seated patriarchy of Mexico, where young men were supported, encouraged, and allowed to dream while young women were supported, encouraged, and allowed to dream about marrying one of those men.

Mexican women, however, have been defying the conventional path that was set out for them for centuries. La Malinche was an Aztec woman born into a noble family. Some say she turned her back on her own people by helping Spanish conquistador Hernán Cortés, but given that she was sold into slavery by her own family, maybe her cunning scheme to make a deal with the conqueror was the only way to set herself free.

There was also Sor Juana Inés de la Cruz, the rebel feminist poet from the 1600s who became a nun to avoid marrying a man. She dedicated the rest of her life to writing, existentialist romanticism, and studying 24/7 even though she wasn't in school.

Also, what up to the Adelitas, also known as Las Soldaderas. They were the women who fought in the Mexican Revolution. They didn't show up to tend to wounded men—they fought on the front lines alongside them, and in some cases, led them.

Despite these badass Mexicanas, there is a narrative that many Mexicans, men and fathers in particular, have bought into, which is that men are the protectors of women. These men think it's their job to take care of and provide for women, to make sure we don't step in a puddle, to help us avoid "making mistakes," and to prevent others from taking advantage of us. They believe they must protect us from seeing and hearing certain things, too. In Tampico, where my father grew up, I remember seeing a cantina—like the kind in cartoons or old Westerns with double wooden doors that swing open and closed. The sign above the door read, "No women allowed." Women were not allowed to drink alongside men because drinking was considered unladylike and crass. And, well, it was assumed that women wouldn't be able to prevent what might happen if the men inside were provoked by their beauty. That's the world he grew up in.

I try see this desire to defend women as a form of love. Men want to protect the human beings they love. But this type of behavior can also be controlling and demonstrate an over-the-top machismo that, in the end, isn't helpful because it puts men and women in separate boxes. And then it's hard to break out of those boxes.

One of the things my father worried about the most in terms of coming to the United States was what would happen to his two daughters and his young wife. Mom was still in her mid-twenties when she moved to the United States and therefore quite impressionable. She was also quite gorgeous and therefore attracted the eyes of American men who had seen few Mexican women in real life. In Mexico, Dad had been sold a narrative about American women. They were more independent, and therefore more free. My dad understood that to mean they were also more rebellious in every way.

My sister was a normal American teenager who wanted a boyfriend and also had friends who were boys. This became a huge source of tension within our family.

It probably didn't help that my sister was also gorgeous and stood out because there weren't any other Mexican girls in her high school. She had straight hair, but with deep waves that gave her hair body and volume. She wore hip huggers and tight shirts, miniskirts and black boots, eyeshadow and Mexican earrings. Plus, she had a great smile. A lot of boys liked her and she was cool with that. My father wasn't.

The arguments intensified after we moved to our new apartment and my sister started going out with the saxophone-playing son of the kosher-keeping Jewish family that lived downstairs. Bobby was waiting to see if his number would get called in the draft lottery and whether he would have to go to Vietnam to fight in the war. He was considering becoming a conscientious objector if his number came up.

My dad could not wrap his head around any of this. How was it that his Mexican daughter had a Jewish boyfriend? A white boyfriend? A Black boyfriend? Or any boyfriend she wasn't planning on marrying? My father was a brilliant man who dedicated his scientific research to innovating the technology that would give hearing back to the deaf, which was so forward-looking. Yet he was also, in many ways, very old-school and poorly educated on issues of American teenagers, sex, and race. While he might have had reservations about these boys' race or religion, the biggest issue was simply the fact that they were *boys*.

He didn't want my sister near any boys at all. As for my sister spending the evening at somebody else's home, watching a risqué film with a bunch of high schoolers? No, no, no, no, no, no, no. She wouldn't be home until nine or ten p.m.? It was an absolute no in my father's mind.

But my sister was adamant that she wanted to go. Everyone was going to be there. My mom defended my sister. It was just a television show, a movie. How bad could it be? They'll be fine, she said. There will be a parent there. My dad still refused.

Then my mom got the great idea to have Bertha Elena take me, her little sister, along with her. I would be my older sister's chaperone and make sure nothing crazy happened. This arrangement seemed to satisfy my dad and calm his worst fears. He finally relented and said my sister could go as long as she brought me along.

The evening of *West Side Story*'s television premiere, my sister and I arrived at her classmate's gray stone home on the north side of Hyde Park. Teenage boys and girls of nearly every race from my sister's class were there—Black, white, Jewish, Asian. The two of us were the only Latinas. We all gathered around a big clunky television and ate popcorn and potato chips and drank soda pop.

I was the smallest, youngest person there, which made me feel so cool. My sister was never ashamed of me or had a problem taking me anywhere, and I loved her even more for that. I think she understood that she was my role model.

The original *Romeo and Juliet* takes place in fourteenth-century Verona, Italy. Updated to the 1950s in New York City, *West Side Story* is set in the Upper West Side neighborhood of Manhattan. In real life, Italians, Irish, and other European Americans had been living there for a while when Puerto Ricans started moving into the neighborhood.

By the way, it's not like Puerto Ricans, who are American citizens by birth, just decided to fly to Manhattan. The island is a colony of the US according to the United Nations, and Puerto Ricans came to New York after being enticed or recruited or forced off their island. The communities in this specific neighborhood were boxed up and kept separate. In the movie, each ethnic group had their blocks that they lived on and controlled, which was enforced by two fictional gangs, the Sharks and the Jets. The Sharks were the Latino Puerto Rican gang. The Jets were the white gang.

West Side Story challenged the social norms of the time around who was allowed to fall in love with whom. It's about borders. Just as there were borders between neighborhoods, between rich and poor, white and Black, between Mexico and the United States, there were also borders being drawn around who people could love.

Even though the story was about Latinos, there were barely any Latino actors in the entire film. Puerto Rican actress Rita Moreno won a supporting actor Oscar for her role, but the main Puerto Rican kid and leader of the Sharks was played by George Chakiris, a Greek American actor. Most of the actors playing Puerto Ricans were forced to wear thick orange pancake makeup to make them appear dark, which now looks very strange to modern viewers. Racism finds its way into everything, folks. The film was supposed to show how foolish and harmful racism is, but at the same time, it played into another kind of racism that said Puerto Rican actors couldn't be in American movies based on the belief that Americans wouldn't pay to watch Puerto Ricans on screen. The director himself couldn't see them as human.

Once the movie started, the room went silent. Everybody was deeply engrossed in watching the film. Nobody made a peep because we couldn't pause or rewind the movie if we missed something.

I didn't know much about the movie before I watched it. In fact, I was totally surprised when Tony, the lead white guy, falls in love with Maria, the lead Puerto Rican girl, and sings the most beautiful song that begins, "I've just met a girl named Maria." Well, I have to say that song made me fall in love with myself a little bit. In the same way that our annual family trips to Mexico were teaching me about my roots and building my sense of identity, watching *West Side Story* was like an act of self-love because it made me feel visible.

The character of Maria was played by a white actress named

Natalie Wood who was definitely not Puerto Rican. But I kind of imagined that I looked like her, with her dark hair and eyebrows and fuller lips. And, of course, she had my name.

I didn't cry tears of joy right then and there because I was surrounded by a group of teenagers, but that's definitely how I felt on the inside. I was beaming with a feeling of pride and recognition. *Oh my god, I exist. Maybe now I'll be able to get a keychain with my name on it.* Having a keychain with your name printed on Plexiglas was the in thing, but none of the keychains ever had the name Maria on them. If there was space for Maria in *West Side Story*, then maybe there was also space for a Maria like me in the real world. That film opened up a world of possibilities for me. Maybe I could have a boyfriend like Tony one day, too.

When you feel invisible because you don't see yourself represented in popular culture or the media, it makes you think that many things are not possible for you, and it's bad for your mental health. Aside from the actor Freddie Prinze, there were almost no Latinos in television or films when I was growing up. Can you imagine near total invisibility in all forms of media?

But just seeing Latinos represented in *West Side Story* didn't solve everything. Instead, it raised a lot of questions that I didn't completely understand. Why were the Latino kids in a gang? Why did Puerto Rican people move to New York City in such large numbers? Why did their accents sound so strange? Why weren't there any Black people in this movie version of New York?

The film planted other questions in my mind as well. There

was a song called "Gee, Officer Krupke" that seemed to question the police and how they treated young people. The movie painted a picture of New York City as this gritty, cool place. Leonard Bernstein, who wrote the music, was Jewish. Later I learned that he had a profound respect for Puerto Ricans, Latinos, and Afro-Caribbeans. He was inspired and touched by much of the Yoruba-Santeria religion and experience when he wrote this beautiful, though very time-stamped, piece of work.

The entire time I sat watching the movie I felt a current of electricity flowing through my body. I was so excited I couldn't even eat the popcorn, which is one of my all-time favorite foods. My eyes barely blinked because I didn't want to miss a thing. I felt like I was being hypnotized and transported to a city I had never been to before, but I could feel those cracked sidewalks under my feet. When the credits ran, my sister and her friends jumped up and started being teenagers, but I just stayed there and watched till the screen went black. This moment changed my life—and it wasn't just me.

Television created the possibility of a national communal experience. Everyone across the entire country would be watching the same thing together at the same time. But there was a downside to that, too. It also meant that there was limited space for the kinds of stories that made it on air and often these narratives were one-sided, increasing certain communities' invisibility like, for example, Mexicans, Latinos, and immigrants. I mean, think about it: The newsrooms and writing rooms where TV shows were created were made up almost entirely of white men. Back then, I thought this was just the way things naturally were. But later I realized that *all* of the media is owned by white men, many of whom are very nice indeed, but they see the world from their perspective. It's just their side of the story that we are getting.

Like most kids, I watched *The Brady Bunch*, yet I knew my family was nothing like them. When the show *Julia* came on television in 1968 about a Black woman who works as a nurse, it was a huge deal. It starred Diahann Carroll and was the first series to feature an African American woman as a lead in her own prime-time show. I loved that show because there were many Black nurses in my neighborhood who worked at the same hospital as my dad. For me, *Julia* was a neighbor who finally had her own TV show. It lasted only three seasons.

When I went back to school the day after *West Side Story* aired, everyone was paying attention to me because they had all heard my name blared out across the nation. My classmates gave me a thumbs-up because there was a song about me. Kids sang that song to me. Some of them teased me. The attention felt strange, since I hadn't done anything different. I definitely loved my name more after that night, but in the movie Tony had died because he loved a girl named Maria. So yeah, it was confusing.

My life can be broken into two periods: before *West Side Story* and after. It changed the way I saw myself as a young woman, as a Latina, as a Mexican, as somebody who speaks Spanish, as a human being. I had heard my name belted out over the airwaves. Everybody in the entire country who had access to a television had seen the movie, had seen and heard Maria.

Maria was not a common name in Chicago at that time. When I introduced myself, people often responded, "You mean Marie?" Now I knew I could say, "You know, like Maria in *West Side Story*," and everybody would know what I was talking about.

But when I was alone, I knew that I had almost nothing in common with the Maria in the movie. I was not Puerto Rican. I had never been to New York. I didn't live in a segregated community. I didn't know what it was like to be in a gang. My mom did not work in a garment factory. Even though Maria's existence made me feel visible, I also understood that the narrative was all wrong. It wasn't my story.

CHAPTER 11

Growing Pains

West Side Story had another kind of impact on me: It made me want to become an actress. I wanted to be the Maria in the movie—the actress Natalie Wood. I wanted to sing and dance on film. I felt like that was what I needed to do to be visible in the world.

When the seventh-grade teacher Mrs. Petzold decided on her own to create a theater department at Bret Harte, it changed everything for me. Soon I discovered that I loved the whole process of being involved in a theatrical production: the challenge of learning all your lines, the fear you feel about performing in front of an audience, the camaraderie of working together with your classmates, the creativity of building a set from the ground up and transforming a space, the joy of making people laugh. The thing I loved the most was feeling like I was part of a team that was working together on something fun.

The first show we put on was Shakespeare's *Macbeth* when I was in fifth grade. Mrs. Petzold directed the whole thing. She was a teacher and an artist, creating something out of nothing but inspiration. She cast me as one of the three witches. Right before I went on stage, I could feel butterflies in my stomach. I realized that I was capable of eating those butterflies for lunch, that I had the capacity to push through. Even though I was afraid, my fear never made me buckle and instead gave me the ability to focus. It made me realize that there was something bigger than me pushing me onto that stage. Because, heck yeah, I was terrified, but somehow I still did it. And that was incredibly affirming and exhilarating. Attempting to become someone else as an actor on the stage was also teaching me how to become more of myself in my day-to-day life, and teaching me how to act as if I felt like I really fit in, even if I didn't.

I became friends with a lot of the girls in my class, and friendships I'd had since elementary school deepened. Susie, Mary, Elizabeth (who now went by "Liz"), Teresa, and Derek had all gone to Bret Harte with me, but now I got to know more about them. Susie's parents were both psychoanalysts. Teresa had a single mom, and so did our newer friend, Leslie, who was white. Caren had an adopted sister from Korea. Rachel's parents were scientists. Jane was born with several fingers missing. Derek and Emmett had a new friend, Paul, who was Black like both of them, and the three were my closest boy friends.

Around this time, a girl from Japan arrived and joined our classroom, and finally I was displaced from being the smallest in the class. Welcoming this new classmate was my first attempt at expressing solidarity with someone who was smaller and less powerful than me, which became a kind of life motto.

In fifth grade we had to learn sex education, which brought our class together in a way. Nothing can bond a class more than having to go through that awkward experience. We were all getting older. I watched as some of my friends started getting meaner, too, and I didn't know why.

By now, I understood that I was a good student. I worked hard and I got E for Excellent on all my report cards year after year. Getting good grades felt like proof that I belonged even though I wasn't American and English wasn't my first language. I knew my parents expected this from me and I wanted to make them proud. My dad was such a serious scientist, and I liked seeing his big smile and getting a hug from him after he saw my report cards.

Around this time, some of my classmates started calling me "teacher's pet," as if I were a perfect student who thought she was better than everyone else. My fifth-grade teacher, Mrs. Eisner, was a nice Jewish lady who cared about her students and treated us well, even if she did yell a little bit too often. She had a raspy voice because she smoked at least a pack of cigarettes a day. There was no reason to think I was her pet, but that's the rumor that got around.

One day I had to stay late after school, and Emmett and Derek stayed behind and waited for me to come out. Then they taunted me the entire way home. I tried to walk along an ice-covered sidewalk while they shouted at me, "Nobody likes you! You're the teacher's pet and everyone hates you! You're an ugly midget, shorty!"

I was wearing a long striped scarf with fringe on the ends because that was the style. Emmett and Derek each grabbed one end of the scarf and began pulling it tighter and tighter around my neck, choking me as I gasped for air. It was painful and terrifying. I started crying uncontrollably and went limp because I couldn't fight back anymore. They got scared then and ran away, leaving me in a pile on the frozen sidewalk.

I told my mother what had happened as soon as I got home. She called up Emmett and Derek's mothers, the boys apologized, and we moved on.

I had been in school with Emmett and Derek and the rest of my classmates since kindergarten. We cared about one another. We had grown up together and lived through a lot— the assassinations of JFK and MLK, civil rights demonstrations and anti-war protests, a teacher's strike in Chicago that had kept us out of school, and police swarming our neighborhood. We had lived through beautiful things, too, like the opening of Bret Harte's theater department and putting on shows for our parents, and enjoying concerts from visiting musicians and lectures by important speakers who came to our little school. We had experienced all of that together. But now we were growing and changing in different ways.

I'd been noticing boys since kindergarten and thought some of them were cute. There was Tommy with his big smile and those rosy cheeks. Michael with his dark eyebrows. And Jonathan who wore glasses and beat-up tennis shoes, which I thought was endearing. Most people saw gender identity and attraction in a much more rigid way back then. According to society's rules, you were either a boy or a girl, based on the body parts you were born with. If you were a boy you were supposed to like girls, and if you were a girl you were supposed to like boys. Most people weren't open to the idea of identifying in a different way or liking someone for who they are, not because of their gender.

These crushes were all before the fifth grade. We never even held hands. All we did was write little notes on pieces of lined notebook paper. We folded them into intricate little packets and passed them from one student to another until they made it to the intended reader.

But in sixth grade, I was invited to a birthday party after school at a friend's house. I had played spin the bottle once before, but at this party we were going to play "two minutes in the closet," where a boy and a girl would be sent into a closet alone to do whatever they wanted. I never knew where this game came from, but the boys loved to talk about it. Everyone assumed they would make out. I was petrified. I hadn't really liked how it felt when a boy kissed me the first and only time I played spin the bottle. Of course, it had been a boy I didn't like. Still, I was convinced I wasn't going to like what was about to happen. I wished I had said I didn't want to play, but I didn't want to be made fun of.

I felt pressured to go along with the game. The general sentiment was that if you didn't join in, there must be something wrong with you. This is not the way to find a friend who you like in that way, and it's why so many of us suffer and feel forced to go along, which is not normal. I also thought that doing "two minutes in the closet" would help define me as being more of an American girl. American women were open and explicit about their sexual desires and needs; they weren't shy about kissing a boy for two minutes in a dark room. It felt as though I was competing to prove I could be more American than the other girls in my grade, who I'm sure were not aware they were part of such a competition.

When it was my turn, I went into the closet with my friend Mark, who I liked. He was sweet, but the sensation of his tongue touching mine felt strange. I wasn't sure I liked it very much at all, but I survived the game.

As my relationships with boys were changing, so were my relationships with girls. In sixth grade I learned the word "ostracize." The verb "to ostracize" means to exclude someone from a group, to reject, ignore, or even ban someone. When a person is ostracized, they are the one who is excluded, rejected, and ignored. That year, I was ostracized by some of my classmates.

Out of the blue, my close-knit group of girl friends turned on me. They stopped talking to me and treated me like I had been touched by leprosy. This was a lonely time in my life. I cried a lot. My mom tried her best to soothe me, but all she could say was, "You know what, mamita, they're just jealous of you." I'd give her a look that said, *That's not the answer I need right now.*

The truth is, I didn't know what I needed. This was such a new emotion. I felt so lonely and scared and out of balance, like I was dizzy. My friends weren't talking to me and suddenly I was all alone. How could I face the world by myself?

This made me feel angry, which made me want to be mean to someone else. Meanness is a cycle, and you can easily choose to pass it on. During this period when I had no crew and was struggling, I came upon a group of kids who used their meanness to look cool.

This new group of girls were a lot more rebellious, more feminist-minded, 1970s cool-independent, and anti-authority than I was used to. These young women, all of whom came from single-parent families, did what they wanted mostly because their one parent was busy working and not watching them. I was twelve years old when I tried smoking pot with them for the first time. Though I barely inhaled, we were too young to be experimenting with marijuana. I also ditched class for the first time with this group of girls. But of course, I got caught. That's the thing about ditching—you will eventually get caught, so it's not really worth it.

My parents gave me a stern talking to when they found out I had ditched class (luckily, they never found out about the pot). They said I wasn't showing them respect, and that I needed to learn how to respect boundaries, and according to them, there was no way I was going to learn those values hanging around American kids. After the last day of sixth grade, I was shipped off to Mexico for the summer, along with my brother Jorge as a chaperone, to live with my aunts and uncles and learn to be a more proper girl, pues more *Mexican*, like not disrespecting your parents by cutting school with your anti-authority friends (to which I was like, *But it had nothing to do with you, Mom and Dad!*).

In the end, cutting school changed my life because those months I spent in Mexico changed my life. In Mexico City I would wake up to the sounds of the mailman with his tiny pan flute and the garbage man ringing an actual bell from his truck. In Guadalajara I fell in love with my cousin's neighbor José and tried my hand at flirting in imperfect Español. I worked at styling my Sears catalogue clothing to look as cute as the fancy dress-up boutique threads that my blond-haired, blue-eyed cousins wore to stay competitive in the status-conscious city of Guadalajara. In Tampico on the Gulf Coast it got so hot that the asphalt under your feet felt like it melted every afternoon. Our only entertainment was to walk forty minutes in the sun to the one ice cream shop in the city with air conditioning. It was called (in Spanish please) Superrrrr Creem!

This time in Mexico, with my brother and me bouncing around various family members' homes without our mother, was one of the most important times of my childhood.

I learned to trust Jorge and realized that he actually loved me and wanted to take care of me. I learned I could live without my parents. I learned that we could travel alone, that people treated us with respect, that my Spanish was good enough for me to make it in Mexico. I felt more Mexican by the end of our stay than when I had arrived. In fact, I was a little obsessed with measuring my Mexican-ness. How Mexican was I? How American? What was the ideal balance that I wanted, the best percentages? As if that existed!

Much as I enjoyed that experience, I still never felt like I was pretty enough or smart enough or spoke Spanish as well as my Mexican cousins. The feeling of not being good enough seemed to follow me everywhere, no matter what side of the border I was on.

But the experiences I had in Mexico made the transition into seventh grade back in Chicago much easier. I felt grounded. More centered. More respectful of my parents and filled with love for my family on both sides of the frontera. And now I had the best style, with all my one-of-a-kind pieces from Mexico, including hand-me-downs from mis primas.

By the time I made it to eighth grade, I was coasting. I had made peace with all the people who had set me aside. I had my time in Mexico under my belt, a growing sense of the person I wanted to be, and high school to look forward to. I'd made la paz with my grammar school experiences. I had one best friend, Liz, and that was enough.

I felt I had made an imprint on my school and people knew who I was. I was a cool eighth-grader who acted on stage. I was proud of being different, but also, I was just like everyone else. On one of our last field trips that year, we went to the Museum of Science and Industry. We put on a talent show at the auditorium. I wore a triqui huipil, a simple woven dress traditionally worn by Indigenous women in Mexico, and I recited poetry from Pablo Neruda, the Chilean poet and defender of human rights. I was in the beginning stages of owning my Mexican-ness. This deep desire to find myself and carve out an identity on my own terms was part of the culmination of eighth grade for me. I was getting ready to graduate from Bret Harte and say goodbye to all the friends I had been going to school with since I was five years old.

I found strength and confidence in what had always made our school and neighborhood special. Thankfully, I was part of a community that accepted me for who I was, allowed me to be proud of what made me different.

At the end of the school year in 1975, my classmates and I celebrated our imminent graduation by writing jokes and doodles and heartfelt goodbyes in each other's autograph books—a kind of notebook people used to collect autographs. Some people carried these notebooks around with them to concerts and asked famous people to sign them. Students like me used them at graduation time so we could ask our friends and classmates to write a message to remember them by.

I got to take a look at my autograph book recently for the first time in many, many years. On the front of the book is my name engraved in bold gold lettering. Inside there are pages and pages of autographs from my teachers, the principal, and all my best friends at Bret Harte. There are pictures of my classmates, too, taken by the school photographer.

My friend Carrie, who included her school portrait, wrote, "I don't know why you want this picture. I hope I don't really look like this."

From Clarence: "To one of the finest chicks I know and one of the best friends I've had. Good luck."

From Jane, one of the rebellious girls: "Well, Maria, what should we be talking about? Ditching? It was a good idea."

From Leslie: "Maria, babe . . . Stay as controversial as you become. It's really a mindblower, but the result always comes out good. Watching you grow is an experience, to put it mildly. Love you too much for my own good."

From my best friend, Elizabeth Takeuchi: "My dear Maria. Wow. What a beginning. Anyway, what can I say to my number one best friend? I mean, you should know as well as I do what I should write. I know that as high school comes, we'll get split apart because chances are pretty small that we're going to go to the same high school, but I want you to remember me as your eighth grade friend. Eighth grade is a really important year because what happens in that year can be important since it can decide a whole future practically. To me, you will always be looked upon as my source of guidance. You are like the sister I never had. And I'll always really be thankful for every bit of help, of courage, of sense, of security just knowing you and you're there that you've given me."

Finally, there is a note from the joker of the group, John. On the first page of the book he wrote, "If you want to read it, turn the page." On the next page it said, "It's too private for the first page, turn to the 197th and a half page." Then all the way in the back of the book there's this note: "I just counted them. And there aren't 197 and a half pages. So this will have to do. Okay, you know, flattery will get you no place. All you have to do is say you love me and get it done with, but I'm flattered anyways. So it got you someplace, where, I don't know thou'st act like a queen upon the stage. It's been a fun fourth, fifth, sixth, seventh, and eighth. Hope you recover from your Elton John sickness. See you at Kenwood. Love John Stein."

My friends and I were growing up. We had been through a lot together but now we were going in different directions. For most of us, graduating and leaving grammar school was the first big separation of our lives. In other ways, we were ready to say goodbye because we knew that moving on would also give us the freedom to become new people: high schoolers.

CHAPTER 12

Looking Privilege in the Eye

After I graduated from Bret Harte, my parents raised the question of whether I would go on to Kenwood Academy, the public high school Bertha Elena had attended and where the student body was majority Black, or follow my brothers to the University of Chicago Laboratory Schools, an elite private school affiliated with the university where my papi worked, which was mostly white. While nobody said this aloud, it was clear that my father felt I would be safest if I went to Lab School with my brothers. My papi had learned and internalized anti-Blackness, and he wasn't alone. Kenwood was being abandoned by families who could afford private school and had the same fears my father did.

Everybody said Lab School was a school for rich kids. I'd already heard stories from my brothers about their classmates getting dropped off in Bentleys. Could I get along well with people who had a lot of money? Would I stand out because my father, a professor at the University of Chicago, got a major discount to send his kids there? I was acutely aware of our class status as an immigrant family. I had to take a test to get into the school and I sweated throughout the entire exam, afraid my public school education had not been good enough. Luckily, I was wrong.

While I was worried about fitting in with rich kids, I hadn't yet realized how different it would be to go from a school that was racially mixed to one that was majority white. The few Black kids at my new school were the richest and sometimes the most status-conscious. I didn't know where I'd fit in.

After being a big fish at Bret Harte, where I had made so much personal progress by the end of the eighth grade, going to the Lab School made me feel like I was in kindergarten again. Everywhere I looked, tall, confident kids whooshed by me with a sense of purpose.

Both of my brothers were big personalities at the Lab School. They had organized a massive student protest that got covered in the local news. But I had not yet been inspired to become a radical activist, as I would be later in college, so my brothers' reputation didn't help me much or clear a path for me to follow. I had to make my own way.

For the first few days at my new private high school, I woke up ninety minutes before school started, at six a.m., when it was still dark out. I would wake slowly, take out my portable mirror, and just like my mami, I would arreglarme la cara, or fix my face. I always used concealer first—I was fourteen, so I'm not sure what I was concealing exactly—then brown eyeshadow, plus black eyeliner pencil lightly on my top and bottom lids, with two coats of mascara after I curled my eyelashes with a strange contraption. The idea was to make my features stand out, not change them, or at least that's what Mami said makeup was supposed to do. Another thing I learned from my mother was that you must never show your face in public unless it's made up. American women went out in our neighborhood without being done up, but not the women in my family. I was especially concerned about looking my best because there was no one else at school who looked like me.

David, my brother Jorge's friend, who was older but also went to our school, already had his driver's license, so he would pick us up in the morning and drive us to school. What nobody knew was that I had already thrown up one, two, sometimes three times before I had even walked out the door.

Every morning before school I'd sit down to eat cold milk and cereal like Frosted Flakes or Golden Grahams. As I ate, I listened to the hustle bustle of the kitchen and tried to remain calm, breathing in and out. Within minutes, though, my nerves would take over and attack my stomach. Then all of a sudden, I couldn't hold it in anymore and I would walk into my sister's bathroom and puke. I didn't want to, but I was so nervous that I couldn't hold any food down.

I was overwhelmed with panic and anxiety, convinced I wasn't going to be able to keep up with my super-rich, super-smart classmates. I was scared of being judged, of not being good enough, of feeling out of place. I didn't know how to name or recognize the issues of race, class, and insecurity that were silently taking their toll on me.

This went on for a month. Day after day I'd find myself back in the bathroom, staring at the toilet bowl after throwing up my breakfast. It was affecting my capacity to focus in class. By the time I got to school, I was starving and there wasn't much time to eat between classes. I couldn't tell anyone what was happening. Just like when I threw up at the beginning of our road trips to Mexico, if I had told my family what was happening, the reaction would have been something like, *That's the silliest thing you've ever done. Stop it.*

My mother hadn't finished high school. My father went to high school in Tampico in one hundred–degree weather and no air conditioning. In contrast, I was sitting here throwing up because I was going to one of the best high schools in Chicago and even in the entire United States of America. *Are you kidding me? We did not leave Mexico for this to happen. Estas safada de la cabeza.* I could already hear their voices in my head. Empathy was not going to be there for me. So I didn't tell anyone.

I realize now these were panic attacks. Nobody used that type of language then. By that age, I knew kids who went to therapy, but it never would have occurred to me that this was something a therapist could help me with. Being anxious and throwing up was not a condition or an illness because I didn't have a name for it. I thought this only happened to me and that meant I had to figure it out on my own.

Eventually, I got so desperately hungry that I started taking my dry cereal in a Ziploc bag with me to school. I'd begin eating it in the car on the way over so that at least I would have something in my stomach, and then I'd slow down my breathing enough to prevent myself from throwing up. Slowly, I was able to piece together a way to crawl out of this debilitating anxiety. Little by little, I started to feel more accepted, relaxed, and calm about being who I was at Lab School. I realized that the other kids who went there were not all a bunch of snobs. There was still a fair share of those types, but it wasn't everyone, which brought me some reassurance.

I forced myself to befriend lots of people. That immigrant voice in my head told me, *Take advantage of every moment that is offered to you because of your privilege. Don't be prissy and take it for granted.* That meant talking to everyone, even kids in the grades above me.

The style at U High (short for University of Chicago High School) was decidedly old school preppy: khaki pants, Izod polo shirts (pink and green were fave colors for boys and girls), and Sperry Top-Sider boat shoes. I happened to look horrible in all those items. Plus, I had decided that unique, special, and different were all good things to be because I was one of a kind. I was the only Mexican girl in my entire school. Slowly but surely, I was like, *Own it, girl, just own it.*

My mom had finally allowed me to wear high heels at the start of high school. I was exploring fashion and developing my own sense of style. The first high heels I got were from Mexico. I started off with one- and two-inch heels, but platform shoes were all the rage in the 1970s. It wasn't long before I was wearing three-inch platform shoes every day. Everybody knew it was me coming down the hallway in stocky platforms.

I was cool with that because it made me stand out from everyone else, and I liked that.

Gradually, as I learned I could be myself and still get along with my classmates, I gained my footing at Lab School. I didn't love the academic pressure or the competitiveness, but I seemed to thrive in that environment. I was willing to work hard to show myself and everybody else that I did, in fact, have the capacity to belong in an elite institution. I was not a straight A student, but I kept my grades up and was consistently a B/B+/A- student.

Lab School made me much more aware of class. I wasn't sure at first why my classmates were working so hard to get the best grades, but by the end of freshman year, I saw seniors getting into fancy colleges and learned what those fancy colleges were—Harvard, Yale, Stanford, Princeton. My classmates' parents, mostly elite intellectuals and professors at the University of Chicago, influenced their college decisions and pressured them to live up to a certain level of prestige. Class differences showed up in smaller ways, too. A lot of my classmates got lunch at the cafeteria, but buying lunch was something my parents could not afford. I brought a sack lunch with me every day and would take it down to the cafeteria to eat with my friends.

To get there I had to pass by the offices of our school newspaper. The truth is, I was fascinated by our high school paper and used to stand in line to be the first one to get it when it dropped every week. The paper was witty and well-written, with good reporting, too. It gave space to important stories and had lots of creative headlines. It even had a comics section with political cartoons. I loved it, but I never imagined I could work there. Sometimes we close ourselves off to possibilities and things we're curious about out of fear. Tienes que comerte el miedo! You have to eat your fear!

I kept looking for a place at Lab School that felt like home to me. In the middle of freshman year, I decided to audition for a student-directed production of *Another Way Out*, a French play set in the 1920s. Because I had been involved in several grammar-school Shakespeare productions, doing theater felt familiar to me and it was something I loved. Unlike Bret Harte, where the teachers had taken it upon themselves to put on plays with the students, my new high school actually had a theater and a dedicated teacher to run the theater program.

I walked into that grungy old theater to audition in my tight jeans, little heels, a flamboyant scarf, and Mexican jewelry with confidence and a bit of an edge, as if to say, *I'm here.* Although I didn't really look like the other theater kids, they all perked up and welcomed me in, as if responding, *Yes, you are. You're one of us.* They didn't see that my knees were knocking together or that I was starting to get that nauseated feeling again. But I rallied for the audition, holding back my knees and my gag reflex, and I got cast as a flirty divorcée.

I did well on stage and I stood out. Getting applause and my picture in the high school paper made me feel less chiquita in the school. This was how I began to have a sense of who I wanted to be in the world of the arts.

Being around other artists helped me begin to open up and blossom, too. I accepted my quirkiness and sought out the other quirkies. My friend Elaine, for example, was a costume designer and never wanted to be on stage. Anderson was a bit of a loner but also a genius. He later ended up spending time in a hospital because he had a mental breakdown. That was the first time I witnessed something like that. Liz looked like me but was Jewish. Together we choreographed a dance where we played each other's shadows. I wasn't in with the cool crowd at Lab School because they were all about getting a perfect score on their SATs, but I moved in many circles, and the theater kids were the most diverse group at school—people from different backgrounds who were questioning and playing with gender norms, sexual orientations, and philosophies.

Our teacher and director for theater class and all the productions was a former professional, and yet it was where people let their guard down and competition took a back seat. My theater friends were less judgmental than the rest of our peers, and part of the reason we were all there was to form a community. Sure, it was still competitive—each of us was vying for plum roles in the next play—but we also spent a lot of our time hugging and hanging out. I liked hugging my friends and the theater people at my school were definitely huggers.

What kept me going and centered me through everything was the thought, *Damn, girl, you are so lucky to be here.* I knew that attending Lab School was a privilege and a choice that my parents had made for me. I heard about that a lot, in fact, because they made it clear they were spending money on our education and, as a result, there was no money to spend on anything else except food and our trips to Mexico. When you're not born in the US, for better or worse, you are saddled with a deep sense of enforced gratitude that gets incorporated into your daily life.

That's why by fifteen, I had a job working at a jewelry store off the books so that I could earn my own spending money. I was following in my sister's footsteps, hired by the historic and now closed Supreme Jewelers for three dollars an hour. Later, I would become a waitress at the famous Medici Pizza, where I learned how to carry a twenty-four-inch deep dish pizza through a crowd. But no matter what I did, I still always felt this restlessness, this gnawing feeling that I should be doing more, or working even harder, or being even more grateful.

I was beginning to become aware of what privilege meant and how it played out. I heard a lot of kids at my elite high school complain about teachers and classes and homework, or worse, not care about anything. In my view, they didn't know how good they had it. That was their privilege showing through. My friend Anderson and I used to sit around and talk about life, philosophy, democracy, and how to get young people like our fellow students to be more engaged. I didn't realize it at the time, but our discussions were also a form of talk therapy to battle his unnamed mental illness. These conversations spurred me to want to take action.

Following in my brothers' radical footsteps, I started an organization called Students for a Better Environment. I tried to take a grassroots approach to getting my fellow students to engage with our school environment as a form of activism. I wanted to push people's buttons, but I was also trying to be conciliatory because the immigrant in me did not want to appear ungrateful, which is like the biggest sin for an immigrant! Our group advocated for more art on the walls of the classrooms and hallways, more student-teacher interaction and spaces where that could happen, more opportunities to shake up the status quo.

I got flack from some of the more conservative students, who said I was being too much of an upstart, maybe too revolutionary. But I wanted to push my fellow students to appreciate what they had. I felt like they were all a bunch of entitled kids who had been going to the same private school since they were five years old. They took a lot of what they had for granted—a computer lab when computers were as big as a mini-fridge, a refurbished gymnasium complex and pool, a new cafeteria, and a beautiful modern campus set against the gothic architecture of the university. I was trying to find my voice as a budding activist for democracy, and for that I am glad. But Students for a Better Environment only lasted about two months.

Eventually I connected with a new group of friends who were quirky and different. I became close to two Iranian sisters, Leyli and Shirin, who reminded me of my Mexican family. We kissed and hugged the way our families did with their friends, though other kids with less affectionate families called us lesbians because of it. They were petite, super well-dressed, and spoke another language at home like me. The tone they used to speak to their parents was different from that of all my other friends. Like me, they showed deference to their father. They were cariñosas, gently affectionate with their mom, just like me. They did not talk back, though I was starting to do it more. Finding a familiar dynamic in my Iranian friends was like finding a safe space where I could exhale and feel understood.

Another friend, Sarah, dyed her hair black and wore it in a pixie cut. She was the first to wear Doc Martens boots to school. She was also very independent. What intrigued me most about her was that she had to make dinner for her family three times a week because both of her intellectual parents believed in socializing the work of a family. Damn! My friend Jenny had just returned from a year in India with her star academic parents who were both anthropologists. She tried to kiss me on the lips once and I didn't want to, but we were BFFs. She and I dressed like boys from India with flowing caftan pants and tunics.

Soon enough, I floated freely between the various social cliques. I got along well with the potheads. I got along well with the jocks. I got along well with the preppies. The place you would always see me most was the dance floor. If there was one thing I looked forward to in high school, it was the dances. I went to all of them. I remember dancing with Michael Dickovitz at a dance in the middle of the cafeteria, which was lit up with purple and pink strobe lights. He touched the back of my neck in a way that almost brought me to my knees. Another time there was an all-day dance marathon that started at eight o'clock in the morning and went until midnight. I was there in the school gym, dancing for sixteen hours in five-inch cork platform shoes. People came to know me for dancing and acting, and I was always down for either.

By the end of freshman year, I was hitting my stride.

CHAPTER 13

Boy Crazy

I was one of only four girls in the entire school who wore high heels.

One of the things I learned intuitively from my mother and other Mexican women was their sense of style, how they made up their eyes, lips, eyebrows, and hair, the way they walked in heels. All of it worked to call attention to themselves. I like to think of it as a form of self-love, the same way Frida Kahlo dressed and made herself up like an art object to walk the streets with pride. But this sort of attention to feminine style wasn't only about self-love. Make yourself the center of attention and you could get someone to notice you—and I wanted a boy to notice me.

In high school, I worked at having a unique look. I did what I could with my sister's hand-me-downs, and with the money I made at the jewelry store and Medici where I waitressed, I could afford to buy clothes in Mexico and at thrift stores. I metamorphosed into a coquettish bird who was always fluttering her wings and saying, *Hey, look at me, aren't I cute?* The competitive girl within me saw myself competing with other girls for boys' attention. And so I decided I was going to get the boy I wanted.

In the big spring play my freshman year I had a tiny role, but the star of the show was a senior. His name was John and he was the preppiest of the preppies. He carried it well, though. His khaki pants looked fabulous on him, as did his pink Izod shirt and his Top-Siders. Everything about him was perfect, especially by the standards of a country that praises tall, lean, white, straight, cisgender, wealthy boys.

The way people of different genders saw and talked to each other was changing. The women's liberation movement had empowered women to take control and make choices about their bodies and their romantic partners. A part of the movement's message was that girls were allowed to openly like boys and even make the first move.

Before I got to high school, I kept any "boyfriends" I had secret from my father. Boys were never to be discussed in front of him, not even in a joke. But my father trusted me more than my sister because I was always hanging out with my brother Jorge. As my older brother, he could look out for me, so in my father's eyes, I was safe.

Just before high school, I started a relationship with a boyfriend who was older than me. Peter was a high school sophomore when my brother introduced me to him. His parents were German, so he spoke German at home and his family ate their cheese omelets with jam on top, which I thought was quite a German thing to do.

Peter and I got along intellectually. He was a budding anthropologist and archeologist who spent his summers on digs sifting through artifacts left by the Indigenous peoples of southern Illinois. He would write me ten-page letters by hand. I liked being alone with him; he was gentle and sweet. Our physical attraction didn't really go much beyond kissing. Yet our relationship caused me a lot of inner turmoil. We only saw each other outside of my home, and the relationship didn't last long.

Then freshman year I got a little too close to one of my brother's friends. He liked me and was very sweet. Well, the next thing I knew, I had a big hickey on the right side of my neck, which felt gross when it happened. I had to wear a scarf every day for a week.

One morning, Mom walked into the bathroom when I didn't have a scarf on. It was not a pretty scene. She used a word for me that I will never forget. I know she didn't mean it; she was caught off guard and was terrified. Her fourteen-year-old daughter had been smooching with a boy and was showing it off right in front of her face. According to my parents, making out with a boy was not something to be celebrated, it was something to be feared. I think my mother knew I was not about to marry the first boy I kissed, and so my involvement with boys worried her on multiple levels. All she could do was draw from her own experience of kissing one boy and then marrying him.

A part of me felt that I was doing something wrong. Hanging out with secret boyfriends meant I was disrespecting my family, and I lived with that every day. I walked around with a lot of guilt. But I also enjoyed this little streak of independence and was curious about my own body.

By the middle of freshman year—after I had long since broken up with Peter, lost interest in my brother's other friends, and had my little escapade of afternoon delight with the boy who left the hickey on my neck—I had gained enough confidence and experience that I felt I could do what I wanted (mom and dad's disapproval notwithstanding).

John, the preppie who played the lead role in my first theater production, could not have been more different from me. He came from a family of bankers and they lived in a huge house in Hyde Park. His eldest sister was famous because everybody in school knew she had earned a perfect SAT score. What was I, this short, flat-chested girl with crazy curly hair, doing going after this straitlaced white boy?

But he was the guy I decided I wanted. Chasing him would be a test to see if I had perfected the art of flirting from all my time spent watching women in Mexico. I won him over by laying the coquettishness on thick and, well, by trying to be myself. We spent a wonderful summer together just before he went off to college, exploring our lives and dreaming about what we would do in the future. There was an assumption between us that we would be together for decades to come. We had planned out our entire lives. He would work at a bank in New York, and I would work at the United Nations.

During all our time together, we were rarely around his family. I met John's mother only once. I had heard the term WASP—white Anglo-Saxon Protestant—before and now I was coming to understand what it meant. And I knew I was not one. I did not feel welcome or seen by his family. I felt like I was never going to measure up to their WASP standards.

By contrast, John was always welcomed into my home. My mom loved John and would give him big kisses that would make him blush. His peach cheeks would turn bright red, as would the back of his neck. He loved sitting in our crazy flower-wallpapered kitchen and listening to the ratatat of Spanish mixed with English spoken back and forth across the dinner table.

The only times I went to his house were when his family wasn't around, so everything we did was secret. It was still fun, but it felt clear that I was not "bring your girlfriend home and introduce her to your parents" material in his eyes. I began to doubt myself. I never asked John why he didn't invite me to spend time with his family. He probably would have said he had no clue I felt excluded and less than, but sometimes that's what privilege looks like. Sometimes privilege makes someone oblivious to other people's suffering and blocks them from understanding what it's like to be a woman of color, a Mexican, an immigrant, a Latina. We live with a lot of insecurities in an overwhelmingly white-dominated America. So if you feel unsure of yourself, that's a normal way to feel, even if it's not fair or just.

In the fall, John went off to Wesleyan, a fancy East Coast

college, and I began my sophomore year of high school. It was hard managing a long-distance relationship. I spent a lot of time on the phone that hung on our kitchen wall. The only way to get any privacy was to go as far away as the length of the curly plastic phone cord would allow. In December, a few days before my family was planning to head off on our annual road trip to Mexico with all six of us in the car, driving through the wintry highways of the United States of America, John and I had a conversation about what we were doing over the holidays.

I was explaining to him what it was like to cross the border into Mexico by car and how when we crossed back into the United States, I would have to show my green card to get in. This, for some reason, didn't make sense to him.

"Why?" he asked.

"Because I'm Mexican," I answered.

"You're not Mexican. You're American."

"I mean, I am in the sense that I live here. I speak English. But I don't have an American passport."

"What? No, no, no, you're American," he kept insisting.

Nowadays you might call this mansplaining. I didn't have a word for it then, but every time he argued that I was American, I felt like he was taking away and dismissing who I was as a proud Mexican. My parents instilled that pride in me. Even though I wanted to be a part of the United States of America, I was also proud of being Mexican and Latina.

I didn't understand why John wanted to take that part of my identity away from me. Did I have to pull out my green card with the squiggly lines that said "Resident Alien" to prove it to him? I was not an American citizen. Why couldn't he understand that? And if he couldn't understand that, did that mean that he couldn't see who I truly was?

This was a deeply impactful moment that left me confused. Everything about our conversation revolved around my identity. The concept of intersectional identities in which race, nationality, gender, and many other things converge was not something that was widely talked about when I was growing up. People talked about the experience of being Black in America, and the issue was being advanced by the Civil Rights movement. As Mexican immigrants we understood some of that and saw how it might affect us. But there wasn't yet an awareness of what I was experiencing as an immigrant, a Mexican, and a Latina living in two worlds. The idea of a Latino identity didn't exist yet.

Instead, we had the word "Hispanic," which I really didn't like. The term was adopted by President Richard Nixon's administration in the 1970s and then legitimized by the census in 1980. On the one hand, it was useful because it allowed the Census Bureau to create a category that would more accurately account for people from Latin America and help set aside resources for those communities. In fact, the National Council of La Raza had lobbied to get "Hispanic" added to the census.

On the other hand, the word is a misnomer and is based on the idea that Hispanics are a people united by their Spanish-speaking heritage. But that overlooks the fact that Spanish is the conqueror's language and Latin America is home to millions of

Indigenous people who only speak Spanish today because they were forced to by the conquistadors who arrived from Spain.

I broke up with John soon after that conversation. I wanted a boyfriend, but not at the expense of this other thing that was so profoundly important to me—my identity, my *who am I?*, my *I'm proud of being who I am* self.

During spring break my junior year of high school, I had saved up enough money from my waitressing job to buy a plane ticket to visit a friend in London. I traveled through Scotland and Wales, continued on to Paris by ferry, and then took a train to Nice where one of my high school friends was an exchange student. This was my first trip traveling alone through foreign countries and it was exhilarating. I was growing into an independent woman who had the courage to travel anywhere and make friends with anyone. I didn't need a boyfriend to have a good time or to be the truest version of myself.

CHAPTER 14

The War That Nobody Wanted

As I made my way through what felt like very long school years and way too short summers, the chaos of the outside world continued to swirl around me and my family. We never knew what we would see when we turned on the television. The war in Vietnam raged on. It was like an open wound festering without the proper treatment, and it became a source of trauma, rancor, and sadness for the entire world.

For us—my family, my school, my neighborhood—the war was personal. I knew people (older than me, of course, but not by much) who had gone to war. Every day the evening news aired images of soldiers being shipped off to the front lines of war, young men fighting in the thick jungles of Vietnam, and body bags carrying the dead being unloaded from planes. My brothers couldn't be drafted because we were not American citizens, but that didn't make us any less against it. We did not want a war against anyone.

Media coverage of the Vietnam War was brutal, and because it was relatively unfiltered, it was more honest than anything we'd seen before on TV about a war. It was the first war to be televised, so the government gave journalists near-complete access. Everyone thought this was the way it was supposed to be done on TV. Just show it all.

You, my dear reader, have probably never seen graphic images like the ones we saw because they're no longer allowed to be shown on television. But it was those same images that inspired the public protests that finally ended the Vietnam War.

The journalists covering the war in Vietnam took their cameras into the front lines and told the ugly truth about it. That truth was presented to the American public every night and it led people to protest. I began to understand the impact of journalism. Educating people and giving them facts generated different kinds of responses. Some people took to the streets, some people went and voted, some people wanted to educate themselves more and went to college.

Why was the US attacking people in a place called Vietnam? The TV showed us images of mothers, babies, and children crying. Photographers captured pictures of Vietnamese people in terror for their lives at the hands of American soldiers. Images of the landscape showed a country that was beautiful, green, and luscious—a picture of tranquility until the bombs and explosions started again.

I heard a lot about "the enemy," the Viet Cong, and places I had never been to like Hanoi, Laos, and Phnom Penh in

Cambodia. The Viet Cong had to be stopped and their soldiers had to be killed because the US government said they were a threat. When I saw a photograph of a little Vietnamese girl running naked toward the camera, her body ravaged and burned, napalm dripping from her delicate fingertips, on the front page of *The New York Times*, I was shocked and ashamed. Her name was Phan Thi Kim Phúc and she was only a few years younger than me. Her small, preadolescent body reminded me of what I looked like at that age. I realized she could have been me. She was not my enemy, nor were any of the Vietnamese.

The news media talked about Vietnam constantly, and yet we never actually heard from the Vietnamese people themselves, never heard them speak their truth. As a family of Mexican immigrants, we could identify with that feeling of erasure and invisibility. We never heard someone with a voice like my father's thick Mexican accent talking about scientific theories on television either.

We had seen racial hatred in the US on TV: angry white men and women yelling and screaming at Black people for protesting for their civil rights and threatening the young white people who supported them as allies. We also saw the racial hatred against the Vietnamese people. Neither made any sense. Why were we sending young men to go off and fight in this war? The horrendous fact that thousands of people, Vietnamese and Americans, were dying for nothing was inescapable.

President Richard Nixon may not have started the Vietnam War—in fact, he said he had a plan to end the war—but he received the most condemnation for it and all the other things he did to tarnish the office of president.

My brother Raúl had a huge poster hanging on the back of his bedroom door that showed Richard Nixon sitting on a toilet and smoking half a joint, looking terrible, his face wrinkled and gross, his pants down at his ankles, all while saying, "I'm not a criminal." It was almost phosphorescent, and quite disgusting, but it symbolized what we came to think of American politics in general, and specifically President Nixon.

When Nixon, the incumbent Republican president, won the 1972 presidential election against Democratic candidate George McGovern, it was the first time I experienced the gut punch of an election loss. Out of my entire family, only my father could vote and he voted for McGovern. I didn't know much about the voting process or how decades of voter suppression had kept Black people from casting their ballots. The people I knew in Hyde Park, Chicago, all voted for McGovern, so how was it possible that Nixon had won? It made me wonder about the people in this country who I didn't know. Electoral politics, I came to understand, was another point of racial division. A majority of white people in America had voted for Nixon.

During the summer of Nixon's reelection campaign for president in 1972, news broke of a scandal called Watergate. At the time I had no idea that it was the name of a building complex. The Watergate in Washington, D.C., was known for its beautiful patios overlooking the Potomac River. Several burglars were arrested for breaking into the Democratic National Committee (DNC) office in the Watergate building.

Nixon swore that he and his White House staff had nothing to do with it.

Then, after Nixon had already been reelected, came the talk of "Deep Throat," the code name of a source who was supplying two journalists, Bob Woodward and Carl Bernstein, with information about the Watergate break-in. These journalists revealed that Nixon, despite his previous claims of innocence, had illegally wiretapped and burglarized McGovern's campaign office at the DNC headquarters. It may seem tame in comparison to what this country has lived through with a president like Donald Trump, who consistently and blatantly broke the law, but Watergate was the first case in the modern media era of blatant government corruption. It truly shocked people.

The trial of government corruption was televised. Calls for government probes and public investigations followed. The TV coverage on every channel every day was congressional hearing after congressional hearing. Then, suddenly, tapes of the president's most private conversations surfaced. We spent our evenings listening to the voice of Richard Nixon on gravelly cassette tapes. A lot of it was bleeped out because Nixon, it turned out, had a potty mouth. The President of the United States, the man who portrayed himself as holier than thou, as a protector and a law man, was actually a conniving, foul-mouthed, corrupt human being. Nothing like this had been televised before and it was riveting.

In Mexico, I was used to seeing political campaign posters plastered everywhere. It seemed like there was always some kind of election going on. But it turned out that my cousins never voted. One of my cousins explained to me that there was only one political party that was going to win, and all the others were shams, doomed to lose to make the favored party look good. The elections were fixed. I did not understand how that could be, even though I generally understood corruption. I understood la mordida. I understood that there was a way to do things outside the law. And now I understood that politics and politicians in Mexico were not respected.

Somehow because I pledged allegiance to the American flag every morning, I believed what that pledge said about "liberty and justice for all." I had bought into the narrative that the United States, its democracy, were exceptional and better than governments in other places. But here was the President of the United States being threatened with impeachment, a word I had also never heard, but came to understand was not a good thing for a president. Unless he wanted to be impeached by Congress and removed from office, Nixon would have to resign.

The news sparked a celebration in our home, and it was announced what time Nixon would be going live on television to make his final statement. It was a Saturday, and looking for any opportunity to hang out with my older brother and his friends, I persuaded everybody to go to Medici where they would be playing the resignation live on the radio for all their customers.

My mom and dad had given me and my brother extra money so that we could splurge and buy our favorite sundaes:

one hot fudge, one Amalfi with whipped cream, both served in tall sundae glasses with toasted chopped walnuts. What made their sundaes special was the hot fudge deposited at the bottom of the sundae glass and the extra dollop on top for good measure. I was digging into one of those just as Richard Nixon said, "I have never been a quitter. To leave office before my term is completed is abhorrent to every instinct in my body. But as President, I must put the interest of America first. . . . Therefore, I shall resign the Presidency effective at noon tomorrow." The entire restaurant erupted in applause. I felt like I was part of a moment in history.

My family had left Mexico for many reasons, but among them was that Mexico wasn't a functioning democracy. We had come to the country that not only had a functioning democracy, but supposedly the best democracy in the world, and now we knew it was essentially a lie. The only thing that made the United States different was that the bad guy actually got caught in the act and had to face the consequences. Still, the US was just like every other place in terms of politics. It was only as good as the people who made it, and any well-functioning democracy needs systems that allow people to participate.

President Nixon's resignation was a defining moment for me. It destroyed the illusion that we didn't have to do anything to improve American democracy because it was already so good. Instead of mindlessly repeating the Pledge of Allegiance, I came to question it. Everybody else around me was questioning it too. That was what a good American was supposed to do. Question. Protest. Demand better. If we wanted to make

American democracy live up to its promises, we would have to do something to make that happen.

Journalism was part of that undertaking of wanting to make things better. It was the anonymous source with the weird name Deep Throat, a whistleblower, who gave journalists the information that busted the Watergate scandal open. We never would have known the truth without fearless journalists like Woodward and Bernstein. Speaking truth to power, I was learning, is what democracy looks like.

This was not when I thought, *Oh my god, I think I'll become a journalist.* There were essentially no women journalists telling the Watergate story anywhere. And certainly no Latinas or women of color. I still didn't see myself in the journalism profession because there was no one who looked like me as a role model. Journalists were white men who were praised by everyone else.

People of color did finally start showing up on television, though, whether on *Laugh-In* or *The Jeffersons*. On the popular show *All in the Family*, the racist uncle from Queens played by Carroll O'Connor would call his lefty son-in-law played by Rob Reiner a meathead. This was as close as America got to a confrontation with racism at that time.

Meanwhile en mi casa, politics became el pan de cada dia, as we say in Mexican Spanish, which means "the bread of every day." The protests about Vietnam saturated the culture. The peace sign became the graphic symbol of the moment.

The Vietnam War finally came to its bloody end in 1975. The first televised war was followed by the first televised refugee crisis.

But instead of compassion for people who had done nothing wrong, most Americans disapproved of the government bringing Vietnamese refugees to the US simply because they were different.

The men who ran our newsrooms were white, male, straight, and privileged. With that privilege, they called these refugees, these most vulnerable of human beings who were prepared to leave everything behind and do anything to keep on living, "boat people." That's what it looks like when a newsroom dehumanizes people.

Though I didn't know it at the time, watching the way journalists talked about and talked over the Vietnamese people on television, the way nobody ever asked them to speak for themselves or tell us what they thought about what was happening to them and their country, taught me about the kind of journalism I wanted to do. I wanted to hear from Vietnamese refugees and others who were not allowed to have a voice. Their silence would end up inspiring me to become a journalist. Their silence made me want to speak but it also made me want to listen. Of course, I hadn't fully figured this out yet, but the glimmer of an idea was there.

I would have to get through the rest of high school first.

The family portrait (without my father) that served as our immigration documentation photograph.

Me, just about a year old, sitting in a park on the South Side of Chicago.

Turning 3 years old in Boston, MA. Peep the party dress and my precarious hold on my toy baby.

My First Communion, which meant wearing a white dress, veil, and check out the gloves.

My 7th grade class portrait. I was so self-conscious about always wanting to tame my hair.

My 8th grade graduation, where I was finally given permission to wear big hoops. I haven't stopped since. That deep side part, though!

My high school dance marathon freshman year. I was wearing platform shoes for twelve hours straight. I was in heaven.

Me in a high school play, taking my role as a telephone operator *very* seriously (Karl Wright, who grew up to become a TV actor, is in the background).

This trip changed my life. I was visiting my sister at
her first year in college. It made me realize I wanted
to do the same.

Me and my bro with an early 1980s look.

In my first-year Barnard dorm room breaking the rules with my cat, Che. I was a proud Latina young woman here and so everything in my room was Mexican. I was clearly also obsessed with Che Guevara.

I love this picture of Cecilia and me decked out in the New York City subway. We were hanging out with an Italian tourist that night, who upped our fashion game. The graffiti behind us was everywhere in early 1980s New York!

Before I became a journalist, I was a proud activist. Powerful women taught me how to step up and take the mic. Here I am, leading a protest in Times Square for International Women's Day. I was urging solidarity for Central American women, which I continue to do today through my journalism.

Mom and dad at my Barnard college commencement, June of 1985. The armband I'm wearing was in solidarity with the fight to end apartheid in South Africa.

My best friend David getting ready to drive across the country with me in 1986. we were going from Washington D.C to my new job in San Diego. I had just received my license a month before!

Me, Ceci, and our friend Victoria Tobon at the Botafogo Beach in Rio de Janeiro, Brazil.

CHAPTER 15

Life After High School

High school is a time when many of us devalue our own thoughts and experiences; we think what we have to say is dumb and won't make a difference. I'm telling you now, please don't do that. Each and every thought or idea you have is particular to you. When you say something that comes out of your mouth, your brain, your history, your legacy, your DNA, it has never been spoken before. Why not say it out loud? Why not raise your hand and ask the question?

I had gone into high school wanting to be like everybody else. There were some young women in my high school who were clearly not white, and yet it seemed like they didn't have any kind of issues around identity, ethnicity, or race the way I did. They were able to slip into Top-Siders and khaki pants as easily as my preppy ex-boyfriend. What was the matter with me? Why couldn't I do the same?

The perception was that everybody else was happy, getting

good grades, and had it all figured out. In reality, I wasn't the only one who felt like I was struggling. Everybody wanted to be someone else. This notion of feeling overwhelmed by anxiety, imposter syndrome, insecurities, or depression was all around me and my classmates, but we never talked about it. There were kids who took one too many acid trips and never came back. There were kids checking into what was then known as the psych ward; some came out, some didn't. There were kids we knew who had taken their own lives.

It was scary to see this happening while we were still in high school. Since we didn't have an open dialogue in our school about these things, each of us had to figure it out on our own and fend for ourselves. None of us was aware of the trauma we were living with from witnessing a decade of police brutality, racial hatred, and the war in Vietnam.

On top of that, school itself was a challenge. Lab School was the best private high school in Chicago and one of the top high schools in the country. I loved my classes, but they were tough. School left me, and many other kids, feeling like we were perpetually fighting to keep our heads above water.

To cope, most of us checked out a pair of big, bulky headphones from the library, turned on the record player, and sat down to listen to music to process everything that was happening around us. When the world stopped making sense, at least we could turn to music. I had passed through my Elton John phase and graduated to listening to David Bowie, Earth, Wind and Fire, and jazz by Stanley Turrentine and Dave Brubeck.

Over time I grew more comfortable in my own skin and

learned to embrace the qualities that made me different. I realized that my Mexicanness was what grounded me. I had told myself that I was never going to be like my American classmates, so all that was left was to be me. And as far as my schoolwork went, I had learned from my dad's work ethic that if you want to get better at something, you do it a lot and keep at it. You make a commitment. It was work, work, work, work, work.

One of the best things that I discovered in high school was the library. Since Lab School was part of the University of Chicago campus, we had access to the university's new Regenstein Library that was housed in a modern, chunky glass square complex with multiple floors. There were windows everywhere, stacks of books, reading nooks, and glassed-in conference rooms where you could sit and work quietly with a group of friends.

The library was my refuge, a place where I could go to reclaim a sense of calm from the intense stress of high school. I was there every night starting at eight p.m. and often stayed until eleven-thirty p.m. before heading home. That's where I put in the work every single night to make up for feeling that I couldn't write or didn't understand the material being taught in class, even though I was getting okay grades.

Every time I had to write a new assignment, it was like I had to prove myself all over again. I reminded myself that I had successfully tested into the school. I did belong here. But all my previous accomplishments disappeared whenever I got a new assignment for a twelve-page paper. Sometimes I was asked to analyze the works of an author. Other times it was a paper on political history and I'd hit the stacks to do research and pull out old issues of *Congressional Quarterly* and *Foreign Affairs* magazine. As much as I was afraid of what I perceived to be an intense academic assignment, I was also fascinated. What was this thing called foreign policy? Who wrote for this stuffy magazine called *Congressional Quarterly*?

I immediately enrolled in summer school after freshman year. I was scared of failing and wanted to come up with strategies that would help me. If you feel overwhelmed, what can you do to change that? Find strategies for survival. I had to manage the workload and my insecurities around doing the assignments, so I looked for opportunities at every turn to own my power. I was figuring it out step by step, little by little.

Summer school allowed me to focus on one or two classes at a time. So once summer came, I continued going to the library every day and found a nook or conference room or place in the stacks to put my head down and get to work. I brushed shoulders with college students, master's degree students, PhDs, and law students in the same library and realized they were not superhuman. I was doing what they were doing. Many times people confused me for a college student and that partially helped me see myself as someone who would go to college and continue this kind of study.

There was a part of me that kind of loved summer school. It gave my life a daily rhythm and structure. Each morning I'd get up early to go to my classes and then in the afternoons I worked at the jewelry store, or later, the restaurant. I was always busy—the immigrant in me was always working, always taking on another job, and like my father, finding joy in it.

Our high school had a special program for super smart students who wanted to complete high school in three and a half years. These students went berserk by overloading their course schedule during the school year so that they could graduate early and take advantage of incredible opportunities before heading to college. Some went on to work in labs doing medical research. Others won travel fellowships. What mattered is that they were gone and had moved beyond high school. They were taking the next step.

I was not one of those kids, but it turned out that I had earned so many extra credits toward my degree from summer school that I was eligible to do the same thing. At some point graduating early was discussed with my parents, since it would save them from paying half a year's tuition. If they were okay with me leaving high school early, then I was ready to take the plunge. I hoped that plunge would take me south.

Mexico had been a central part of my identity in grammar school but that part of me went semi-underground during high school. I wanted to get back in tune with my Mexican roots and plant my flag on that side of the border. I'd grown up in Chicago and knew the city well. It was time for me to return to the cosmopolitan metropolis I had been born in, Mexico City.

I designed a project for my post-high school period in which I would leave in January of my senior year and move to Mexico. I found two potential study programs. The first was an arts program in San Miguel de Allende, but it was geared toward Americans who wanted to live in Mexico. Most of the classes were taught in English from the perspective of being an American in Mexico, which would have been really easy for me. Part of what I was trying to understand, though, was that I didn't want to be an American in Mexico. I wanted to be a Mexican in Mexico.

The second option was to take classes with the famed Ballet Folklórico de México at the Palacio de Bellas Artes in Mexico City. I had danced on stage and off throughout high school and made many friendships on the dance floor. I yearned to get in touch with the movement in my body and break out of disco music. Maybe if I learned these centuries-old dances it would help me grasp more clearly what I was feeling, what I was searching for.

Chicago had been the site of many formative moments in my life up to that point. It's where I learned about Martin Luther King Jr., watched the racial tension between Black and white, joined anti-war protests, and experienced boyfriends, high school cliques, and the nightly news on television.

The same was also true of Mexico. Even though I was only in my birth country for five or six weeks a year, a number of life-changing moments occurred there and marked me forever. Some of these moments were beautiful, like the experience of being together with a hundred people, all of them relatives, in one space. Others were more sobering, like realizing I had an uncle who was an alcoholic or learning that my grandfather kept two homes so that he could live with his mistress while still being married to my grandmother.

My Mexican side was still trying to define itself. Just as I felt I was in an unspoken competition with American girls, I also compared myself to Mexican girls. My girl cousins in Mexico ranged from prissy to anthropological researchers, archeologists, and poets. I wanted to be more Mexican like them, and also pretty, smart, funny, and flirty. But above all else, I was determined to be a professional. I was going to have a job, become a career woman, and make my life into something more than just being a housewife.

All my life my parents had been trying to teach me and my brothers and sister about where we came from, which is why they made a point of taking us to museums and archeological sites in Mexico. They were telling me that to understand who I was, I had to go deep, deep, deep into the past. I was ready to follow in their footsteps and explore my own Mexico. What was it? What did it look like? I understood things about Chicago in the United States like how to get around on buses and trains, where to buy groceries, the different neighborhoods that made up the city. But I didn't have that knowledge of Mexico City, my birthplace.

In the end, I proposed moving to Mexico City and doing the program in folkloric dance instead of studying at the American school in San Miguel de Allende. This would allow me to research my Indigenous roots, develop my dance skills, and explore my Mexican identity. My older sister, Bertha Elena, had studied anthropology in Mexico City and Costa Rica during her college years. She, in part, inspired me to do the same.

After I completed the last of my courses in the fall of senior year, I headed down to Mexico with my family for our annual trip. This year my parents gave me permission to spend New Year's Eve with my older brother, Raúl, which was kind of unheard of because he was so irresponsible and usually never wanted to be around me. I had matured, though. The plan was for me to stay on in Mexico after the holidays to begin my classes in Mexico City. Raúl respected my decision and now thought I was cool. He invited me to spend New Year's Eve with him and his hipster friends on a beach in Oaxaca. Because it was my brother, my mom and dad said yes without a second thought.

On New Year's Eve we were out on the beach with a bunch of friends, dancers, and bohemian artists, both European and Mexican. Some local guys thought that because we were on a secluded beach in the middle of nowhere with no one else around, it might be a good time to shake us down for money and other valuables. They robbed us with a pistol in one hand and a machete in the other. It was not a great way to start the new year, but luckily none of us was hurt.

When we called my parents from the police station, though, my carefully made plans of exploring my Mexican identity and Indigenous roots through dance went all to hell. My parents told me I was not as mature as they'd thought, that the incident on the beach was proof that I was not capable of making smart decisions, that I put myself in danger, that I could have been assaulted. They told me they were taking me back to Chicago.

I fought. I pleaded. I cried. I pouted. I gave them the silent treatment. But none of it worked. I was on my way back to Chicago even though I had graduated early from high school. Soon I would be back in my little girl bedroom with the pink flowery wallpaper. I was a heartbroken young woman without a plan.

CHAPTER 16

In a New York Minute

I fought as hard as I could to stay in Mexico. But although I was rebellious and independent, I couldn't just run away from home, much less to Mexico City where the only people I could have stayed with were family who would have forced me to go home. I couldn't leave my parents like that. My life changed directions and I thought, *Well, maybe I'm supposed to go with the flow.*

I got my restaurant job back at Medici and decided to work as much as possible to save up money. I was no longer going to focus on Mexican folkloric dance and so turned my attention back to acting. I had nothing to do, no papers to write, no academic pressure, and I started to think more seriously about acting as a career choice (although I did not share this with my dad).

I paid for entry-level acting classes at Victory Gardens Theater. I was there twice a week with college students, twentysomethings, and older adults who were trying to figure out if they had the talent and ambition to become professional actors. I think my adult classmates loved the fact that there was a high schooler in their midst, and they treated me like an equal. We became friends and hung out. Some of them made it, but I never got cast in any plays.

I also started taking dance classes on the regular, but I didn't get to do any choreographing like I had done in high school. I settled back into my old rhythm. That's exactly how it felt—like I was settling for something and someplace I'd already done and been, as opposed to moving forward dramatically, which was what I thought this time in my life was supposed to be about.

I hung out more with my brother Raúl, who was five years older than me and already starting graduate school. I had really started listening to what he had to say about economic policy, inequality, and structures of racism. He was talking to me about meeting Black jazz artists like Dizzy Gillespie and going to the South Side blues bars like Teresa's and the Checkerboard Lounge. He was hanging around with people who were organizing to run the first Latino and Mexican candidate for public office in the city of Chicago.

I realized that I could cross the border into Mexico without leaving Chicago. All I had to do was find my way back to Pilsen, the neighborhood where I had made those weekend shopping trips with my parents. El Barrio Mexicano was bustling with Mexican Chicagoan Latinas who were making stuff happen. These were women in their late twenties and thirties who had been activists for many years, a reminder that the fruits of activism often aren't achieved in one or two years, but in five, ten, twenty years of dedicated work. They had created an organization called Mujeres Latinas en Acción, Latin Women in Action, and that's exactly what they were. They saw that women in this community were getting abused by men and took action by creating a place where Mexican women and Latinas could be safe and also see themselves reflected as the powerful women, citizens, and immigrants that they were.

I began attending grassroots activist meetings and arts events in Pilsen and my connection to El Barrio Mexicano deepened, but this time on my own terms. My previous experiences in Pilsen had all been dependent on my mom and dad taking me there and being my guides. Without my mom in the supermercado, I don't know what I would have done. I didn't know how to speak to anybody in Spanish the way my mom did. Now I was going there on my own and forging new connections with the people who lived and worked there. Mi gente.

Through my brother Raúl, I was introduced to his friend Beatriz who was a professional activist. Beatriz had been raised outside Mexico City but had moved to Los Angeles as a budding labor activist. Then she had relocated to a city where stuff was happening. If you were into Latino politics then you knew that Chicago was hot and up and coming. Grassroots street politics in Chicago are legendary (remember, that's where Barack Obama got his start).

Beatriz was a savvy organizer focused on organizing Mexican American workers in Chicago to raise their voices about labor rights and to see themselves as part of a binational movement of workers sin fronteras—workers without borders. She was probably a decade older than me, but she treated me like an equal, como una compañera, like a woman.

One day after attending a meeting in Pilsen, Beatriz invited me over for a soda since my brother was going to be late picking me up after attending a day-long organizing meeting for a big workers' rights protest. In her cute little car, she drove us to the residential heart of El Barrio Mexicano. Two flights up, I walked into a space that hit me so hard I got dizzy. I had been in spaces that looked like this before, but in Mexico, not Chicago.

There were political posters next to framed pictures of Frida Kahlo. The walls were painted red and blue and yellow and the kitchen had painted ceramic dishes and cups like in el mercado. There were San Marcos cobijas and different-colored rebozos hanging on the wall next to a Virgencita de Guadalupe. The Virgen had been a symbol for my abuelita, but here in this barrio apartment, she was speaking to me. I was getting to see how a future Mexican, Latina, independent feminist version of myself could build a life of her own.

I recognized pieces of myself in Beatriz, which was fundamental to me figuring out what kind of person I wanted to be. She gave me a concrete visual of what my life could look like, and I liked what I saw. It's strange now to think that a tiny, one-bedroom apartment in Pilsen could rock my world the way it did. I mean, it was just a cute apartment, right? But for me it was a peek into what could be. This visual, visceral, full-body experience touched me to my core.

By the time I was spreading my wings and venturing

out into the world, since I was the youngest of four kids, my parents had been there, done that. They had essentially gone through all of the possible arguments, frustrations, freakouts, punishments, overreactions, and drama of watching their kids become adults. I was a pretty good kid. I had acted in plays that sometimes appeared to be a little bit too risqué for high school. They had caught me with a boyfriend and knew that I had several, but I was not a difficult kid. I was a great student and overall a lot of fun to have around.

Also, my parents were busy. Dad's work on the cochlear implant was really taking off. He was getting closer and closer to making his dream of helping to create a device that would allow deaf people to hear come true. Mom was working hard in the retail clothing store and enjoying her independence and the relative calm with my dad. Going to couples therapy had worked.

During this limbo period, I was waiting to hear back from the handful of colleges I had applied to in the fall. I'd begun to hear classmates talking about the pressure of applying to schools like Harvard, Yale, Radcliffe, Princeton, and Stanford in my junior year. Lab School was a prep school, after all, and the competition was fierce. If you weren't accepted into one of the top colleges or your first-choice school, supposedly that reflected on the kind of person you were, and people really took that idea to heart. One of my classmates who was a straight A student, did everything well, and was perfect all around, got rejected at every single school she applied to.

In my house, my mom and dad didn't put that kind of pressure on us. They expected excellence, and excellence would surely deliver us to a college or university. It didn't matter which one. What we ended up doing in our time in college didn't really matter as much as the fact that we left with a degree. At first I wanted to follow in my sister's footsteps, like in everything, and attend a small liberal arts college, maybe on the East Coast. I applied to Tufts, Hampshire, Barnard, and Georgetown.

Though my family was supportive and I had older siblings to look up to, I remember feeling alone in the application process. I was never good at testing. Any time I had to take a standardized test, I did poorly, usually because I psyched myself into believing that I wasn't good at tests. It was a self-fulfilling prophecy. When it came time to take the SAT, my scores were mediocre. I didn't tell anyone because I was too ashamed. The only other time I'd felt that out of control was when I peed my pants in first grade.

For my personal essay, I wrote about my Mexican identity. I poured my heart out and was as honest about who I was as I possibly could be. I knew I couldn't be like all the other girls from my high school. I had to roll with my uniqueness—that was my strength.

I saved up enough money from my waitressing job to fly to New York and visit a girlfriend who was a freshman at Barnard College, one of the schools I had applied to.

In New York, I fell in love with everything about Barnard and Columbia University. The two colleges sat across the street from each other. Barnard was and still is a women's college, and at the time Columbia was a men's college. I liked the idea of crossing the border between an all-female school into an all-male school.

Columbia's Low Memorial Library was commanding with its massive pillars, and Butler Library was just as impressive. The names of important men were engraved into all the massive buildings, housing complexes, and even individual reading rooms and wings. In contrast, the Barnard campus was small and welcoming. It felt like a close-knit neighborhood in the middle of a big city that reminded me of Hyde Park; it was manageable. But right next door and across the street there were Ivy League preppy boys, Broadway, the subway, and the most dynamic city in the world. I knew immediately that Barnard was where I wanted to go.

My friend Elaine Sahlins, who was the daughter of a super lefty and influential anthropologist and who understood everything about the Ivy League, showed me around Manhattan. One day we hopped on the subway to Times Square and went to see a new Broadway production that had just opened called *Zoot Suit*. It was the first Chicano production to hit Broadway and the first play featuring Latino characters since *West Side Story*.

The story was about the 1943 Zoot Suit Riots in Los Angeles. History books typically describe it as a series of violent confrontations between US servicemen, police officers, and Latino and Black youths. It would be more accurate to characterize it as young Mexicans and Black people standing up for their rights while being targeted by white supremacist police.

Zoot suits were the cool outfits they wore: usually wide-leg pants, sometimes with pinstripes, that tapered at the ankles, a watch chain hanging from the belt buckle and almost touching the floor, starched white shirts buttoned at the neck, and finished with a double-breasted suit jacket with extra-long tails. It was the beginning of serious cholo culture style.

Sitting three rows from the stage, I watched my first Broadway show with my jaw in my hands as I listened to the Latino and Latina actors speak Spanglish like me. My eyes were glued to every single movement on stage. My mouth curled into a huge smile as tears streamed down my cheeks. *Oh my god,* I thought, *this is it. This is what I want to do. This is exactly where I want to be. Can I do this?*

Then I looked at the cast and thought, *What if I'm not Mexican enough?* This was a story about Mexicanas and Chicanas from Los Angeles. But the idea of acting in New York City theater was imprinted in my mind. I could live in New York and go to college. On weekends I'd go see theater and audition for parts in my spare time. I could make it happen. I could become visible by becoming an artist on the stage.

The critics hated *Zoot Suit.* The play had originally opened in Los Angeles where it played to sold-out audiences for nearly a year, but *The New York Times* review panned it terribly. They had no Latinos doing theater reviews or criticism, and their critic did not get any of the cultural references. A bad review from *The New York Times* can often spell death for a Broadway show, which is exactly what happened. *Zoot Suit* closed in New York after only a couple of weeks.

I took the show's failure personally. At the time, I didn't know how to talk about big concepts like media literacy, cultural competency, and representation in newsrooms—the idea that newsrooms should be made up of people who reflect what our country looks like—or why we need critics who come from diverse backgrounds, especially when critiquing diverse artists. I just remember feeling like, *Here we go again.* If people like me wanted to be seen and heard, we would have to fight for it. I was going to have to fight if I wanted to be an artist, to be visible.

Before my trip was over, I went back to see the show two, maybe three times. Tickets were cheap because no one else was going to see it. One night after the show, I was a real groupie and waited outside the theater until the cast came out in their street clothes. I followed them to a nearby bar just to be close to them, to look at them, and see them off stage. All I did was watch them from across the bar. I was still in awe that they were real. I was close enough to touch them. I finally saw a life for myself in this country, in New York City, as an artist. Damn the critics.

I became totally focused on getting accepted at Barnard. After my visit to New York, there was no doubt that this was going to be my city. I loved that it was gritty, grimy, and not polished. I loved that Columbia was in West Harlem, because it would mean being in a community with people from different backgrounds, even if the neighborhood's relationship with the university was complex. Seeing Black people in the neighborhood made me feel more at home, and it was less segregated than Chicago. There were Latinos and Latinas in Harlem, too, and Spanish was spoken on the streets. Being invisible in New York City didn't mean so much because everybody there was trying to be seen.

I loved the fact that the city was open twenty-four hours, that I felt like I could walk anywhere along Broadway as a young woman alone at any hour of the day or night, because there were always lights on and people around. In Manhattan, I felt like I was crossing a border with every block that I walked on, especially on the Upper West Side near Columbia. There would be a doorman apartment next to a small rental building with artists, Latinos, Puerto Ricans, Dominicans, and Black people.

In the spring, I finally heard back from the colleges I applied to. All the notices came in the mail. If you got a fat letter you were in; if you got a thin one, you were out. I got rejected by Georgetown and accepted at Hampshire and Tufts. And there it was one sunny day, the fat envelope from New York City that meant I was in at Barnard.

But even though getting to New York and Barnard was my dream, I soon found myself at a crossroads again.

There was a call for Latino and Latina actors to audition for Chicago's first Latino theater company. Word got around about the auditions in my acting classes. Did I want to go straight to college or take one last detour? I decided to audition and told myself, *If I get the role, I won't go to New York.* I didn't get the role. New York City was about to get another tiny little gusanita in the Big Apple.

CHAPTER 17

Freshman Year

You know those movies where mom and dad pack up their kid and take them to college? They help them with their suitcases and put posters on walls that have had posters pinned up on them by past students for decades? Well, that wasn't my college arrival story.

My parents said there wasn't enough money to accompany me on my move into the college dorm, so I flew to New York on my own. After I arrived at funky lil ol' LaGuardia, the domestic airport sibling to big old JFK Airport, I lugged my suitcases alone to the taxi line and got into a yellow cab headed for Barnard on the Upper West Side of Manhattan. People on the street were yelling at each other with big New York attitudes, the air was crisp but not as frigid as Chicago, and there was a feeling of excitement as everyone hurriedly went about their business. I was under no illusion, though, that New York City would wash away the chaos, racism, and violence I had witnessed in the streets of Chicago.

No, driving through Harlem only confirmed what I now understood: To be Black or Brown in the United States of America meant that our neighborhoods were mistreated, impoverished, and abandoned, not by the people who lived there, but by the institutions and people who controlled them. Garbage pickup came less often, the police were either hassling people for no reason or missing in action when you needed them, the fire houses were understaffed, the upkeep of public parks and spaces was nil. All this contributed to the general feeling of being invisible. Our lives just weren't worth the effort it takes to show some basic respect for the barrio.

I picked up on that same feeling in New York City as my cab drove along 125th Street before turning south toward the Barnard campus. The concept of racial justice had crystallized in my head, and going into college I knew I wanted to devote part of my time to doing something so that people didn't have to live in poverty because of racism. Dr. Martin Luther King Jr. had raised this question for me: Why should people be treated differently just because of the color of their skin?

The cab pulled up to my dorm at 616 West 116th Street off posh Riverside Drive. The building looked like something I had seen in the movies. It was a classic New York City–style apartment building with ten stories made of cement blocks and thick gray brick, the sides adorned with stone filigree, each room with a different story to tell, and there were arched windows on the second floor, too.

As an incoming freshman, I felt that my new dorm was giant and imposing. There were so many apartments, so many windows. But at the same time there was a warmth and friend-liness to it because I would be surrounded by so many women at my college. I wouldn't be alone. That is the way I have always felt about the energy of Manhattan. You are never too far away from humanity.

I got out of the cab and dragged my three suitcases inside, feeling self-conscious but also a bit of that geeky excitement that all first-year college students experience. I smiled awkwardly with twinkling eyes as I grunted and sweated my way up the short stairwell and took the elevator to my assigned room. I would be living in a suite with five other female students. The two upper-class students would each get single rooms, two other students would be roommates in the double room next door, and then I would share the remaining double with a roommate. The suite had one shared bathroom and a kitchen.

When I got to my spot and put down my bags, I did a quick circuit of the suite. It turned out my room was, in fact, the worst of all the rooms in the entire dorm. Maybe they thought I wouldn't complain because I was a "minority" student. Maybe they thought I would just be thankful to be there, which I was. My roommate was a nice, quiet girl from Long Island and the daughter of a French immigrant father. Our room was on the second floor and the only window faced an air shaft that ran through the middle of the building. As a result, it was dark all the time. There was never a breeze nor a ray of sunlight that came through that window, but every single noise from the rooms above, below, and across the air shaft was amplified. We were at the bottom of a dark, cold echo chamber.

Since graduating from high school and spending the last six months waitressing and taking acting classes in Chicago, I had begun shedding the persona who was defined by the high heels and makeup she wore as a young woman. My style had shifted to buying quirky, one-of-a-kind pieces from thrift stores and Army-Navy surplus shops. My new fashion sense was influenced by hardcore anti-establishment punk, *The Rocky Horror Picture Show*, and Fiorucci's, a mod Italian boutique with stores in New York and Chicago where I picked through the sales rack.

I'd buy the strangest looking clothes and throw them together to make an outfit. One time I wore the interior lining of an army jacket as if it were the jacket itself. The heels did not serve me when I wanted to walk long distances across New York City so I traded them for clunky platform shoes and boots. The makeup always stayed with me, though. I couldn't leave it behind, nor my jewelry nor my sense of style. Now I was part of the Latina grunge, Bohemian hipster movement. I had no idea there were more people like me out in the world, but we were and are everywhere.

One of the coolest things about the first days of college and the people that you meet during them is that they may end up being some of the most important moments of your life. Tiny moments can change you forever. That's how I feel about what happened next as I was settling into my dorm room.

My roommate and her parents went out to take care of some paperwork at the administration office, so I was left alone in the room and started unpacking my suitcases. I had not yet met any of my other suitemates. There was a meeting coming up at the top of the hour that we would all go to together. The phone, which was on the wall right next to my door, rang. I swung the door open and picked up the receiver. Back then every phone had a long, curly wire that connected the receiver to the phone box. The person on the other end of the line said they wanted to speak to Cecilia. I imagined that was one of the other people who was living in the suite. I yelled out the words, "Cecilia, there's a phone call for you," and left the door propped open to make sure somebody came to answer.

Then I heard a voice that has stayed with me, almost haunted me (in a good way) my whole life. It was soft and caramel, like an angel's voice, with a particular Spanish accent that made me feel all gooey inside (to be precise it would be Chimbote, dulce de leche caramel). The voice was speaking Argentinian Spanish, dainty yet thick, with a lot of sexy pouting of the mouth and Z sounds everywhere.

It was a sign on my very first day in New York City.

Even though my dreams of studying my Mexican roots and Ballet Folklorico had been dashed, I was still on a quest to embrace my Latina identity and be more intentionally Latina. Right there in my college suite was someone who spoke Spanish. I ripped open the door as soon as I heard her hang up and said, "Oh my god, where are you from?"

In front of me stood a beautiful woman with clear skin bronzed by the sun. She was wearing tennis shorts and a white tennis sweater, and had flowing, light brown hair with a wave I could tell was natural. Her smile was broad and inviting, almost caressing you with its warmth. Cecilia had perfectly white teeth, perfectly straight. Her dark eyebrows looked like they had been colored in, but they, too, were completely natural.

Her beauty left me stunned in the moment.

"Me?" she said, "I'm from New Jersey."

Still in awe of this ray of all-encompassing, head-to-toe beauty, I clarified, "No, I mean, where are you really from?"

"Oh, my parents are from Argentina," she said.

"Wow, okay. I'm Mexican from Chicago. My name is Maria," I said, pronouncing Maria in English.

"I'm Cecilia." She said her name in English too, but a part of me wanted to speak Spanish to her right then and there.

I thought, *Oh my god, she's a queen. The most beautiful woman I've ever seen in my life is living with me. I can't compete with that.*

Soon enough, I gave up the idea of any kind of competition between us. I ended up hanging out with Cecilia a lot over the five or six days of our college orientation experience, which was essentially a week of partying with new friends across the Barnard and Columbia campuses. Cecilia and I became attached like chicle. We made quite a pair: she was statuesque and tanned with long, muscular legs, and always dressed preppy in tennis shorts, while I was tiny in my second-hand clothing from the Army-Navy shops, my curly hair long and purposefully wild, almost punk.

We became sisters very soon after getting to know each other. I realized that Cecilia was in deep mourning. Her father had passed away only a few months before and now she was living away from her tight-knit family, where everyone spoke Spanish. Her mother had a thick accent in English, just like mine did. Cecilia felt out of place in New York City. Sometimes she would disappear for days to go home to be hugged and comforted by her mother. This was how she coped with the loss of her father.

Cecilia reminded me of my cousins, primos y primas, in Mexico who were more like siblings. There was something about the way we understood each other's backgrounds that gave us a kind of unspoken cultural language. Sometimes I would crawl into bed with her and just be there with her, giving her abrazos. This cemented our friendship in a way that words couldn't. Soon we were doing everything together. A central part of our journey was coming into our Latina identities.

During the summer before my transition to college, I had gotten involved with Chicago street and electoral politics by attending a meeting and handing out leaflets. Inspired by my rad brother Raúl, who was a full-blown political activist, I decided that I was going to again continue what seemed to be a family tradition and become an extremely politically aware and engaged person.

I went to an open house event for WKCR, Columbia University's student-run radio station. The only reason I went to the meeting, which was 90 percent men, was because my sister had been a DJ at her college radio station and I thought maybe I could do the same. Also, I was at a woman's college and crossing into the Columbia campus, which at that point only admitted men, was a sure way of meeting some.

José Luiz and Carlos, the Puerto Rican guys in the Latin music department, were cute with their mustaches, goatees, and long hair and they encouraged me to get involved. I stopped by the radio station maybe once or twice that year and read a few news headlines in the middle of their show. I'd stand over the wire machine that spit out the breaking news headlines and rip off anything that had to do with Central America or Latin America. That's why they called it "rip and read." Every time I did this, however, listeners called in to say, "Please put the music back on. We don't want to hear the headlines."

In the end, I couldn't commit to WKCR full time. I was too busy finding my footing, making friends, and figuring out how to survive academically. I was battling a monster they call imposter syndrome and for me that just meant more hours in the library, alone.

I was also trying to figure out what to do about the intense internal conversations I was having with myself about my racial and ethnic identity. Understanding how multifaceted I was led to anger about not wanting to be labeled by a couple of new words that were on the tips of everyone's tongues: "minority" and "Hispanic." I was not less than anyone, so why should I be called a "minority?" I was not going to let my identity be labeled by a government-created term like "Hispanic" either. I didn't want to live with other people's labels. I was a complex woman and human being.

Over the last two years of my high school experience, I had

traveled in Mexico, survived violence when we got jumped on a beach, and explored Europe. I know it might sound corny, but I was like a flower opening up to the world. You know, when a rose or a tulip is tight, they're perfectly straight and closed up? There's something beautiful about that—that kind of innocence. But when a flower begins to open up, that's when it gets its true shape. The petals twist and turn outward and gain more character. I felt like that's what was happening to me. I was in the process of transforming from that very straightlaced, well-dressed young woman with heels into something a little bit louder, angrier, riskier.

The decisions my dad and mom had made in their lives and for our family were big risks. Now, as I came into my own as a radical feminist Latina, I was doing the same. There was something about the energy in New York that I found hopeful, and a little arrogant, curmudgeonly, and creative too.

Everybody in my family had heard the word "radical" because my brother started using it in high school when he became politically active. What did it mean to be called a radical? Was it an insult? Was it something good? I finally looked up the definition for myself. Radical means going to the root of things. I told myself, *I am a radical. I want to go to the root of things and understand this inequality, this poverty, this racism, this sexism, these borders.* You can't change anything unless you go to the root of it.

Being a proud radical also meant questioning everything. My friends and I wore little buttons on our backpacks and our jackets and our coats to express our beliefs and opinions. One of my buttons said "Question Authority." Then, in my first few months in New York, I went to one of the two Spanish language bookstores in the city and got another button that said "Soy bilingue, bicultural, y orgullosa de mi raza." It felt like it had been written just for me. I was bilingual, bicultural, and proud of my raza. Raza in Spanish means race, as in the human race, the people, el pueblo. If you're from the West Coast, raza also refers to Latino and Latina people like Chicanos and Mexicanos. Raza means all of that—I was proud of everything that I was as a human being.

This new version of me had become loud in different ways. My hair was pronounced and unruly. My style called attention to myself. I enjoyed speaking up and being provocative by asking questions. It was a theatrical version of me. It was the artistic me who was finding her voice and trying it on for size.

Sometimes when you're in the process of finding your voice, you have to hear yourself say the wrong thing in order to realize it doesn't sound right coming out of your mouth. You might figure out what you do want to say by realizing what you don't want to say—after you've said it. This isn't the easiest way to learn what kind of person you want to be, but it certainly teaches you to think before you speak.

One of the public events the school put on during our orientation week was a Columbia and Barnard version of *The Dating Game*, a 1970s television show where one man or woman gets to choose from three suitors who sit behind a partition. My feminist college and the 1960s radical men's university across the street were welcoming new students by playing into the most traditional, backward tropes about gender, and in the highest reaches of the Ivy League no less. I was horrified and disgusted.

At one point everybody was screaming at the boy suitor that one of the young women on stage was a "dog," that he shouldn't choose her, and I joined in. Despite my disgust, I got into the game as much as anybody. As a rowdy and sassy (and insecure) member of the audience, I wanted my voice to be heard, regardless of what it was saying. Yet once I heard myself shout those hurtful words about a fellow woman, right to her face, I felt shame. I knew I would never do it again. At that moment, a blond guy in front of me turned around and said, "How could you say that?" I already felt inwardly ashamed about what I had said, and now I was being corrected by a white guy for not being feminist enough? Sometimes it takes making terrible mistakes like this to know you never want to make that choice again.

But even a terrible moment like that can turn into an opportunity to find your people. The next night I ran into that same guy when Cecilia and I went to watch the movie *Columbia Revolts* about the 1968 student protest movement at Columbia University, and we got to talk. His name was David, and we became intellectual, heart and soul buddies. He came from a working-class family in Rockport, a town outside of Boston, and was raised by a single mother. We had different backgrounds, but we connected over poetry, Marx, and existentialism.

As my first year at Barnard went on, my friend group grew, but not by much. Nini was from Iran, just like my high school

BFF Leyli, but Leyli's dad was an academic and was safe in the US. The first stories Nini told us about her father were about him serving in the Shah's military. He later became horrified by the Shah's corruption and theft and had to escape the country by trekking through the mountains of Iran in winter. She still didn't know where he was or if he was going to make it through the snowy mountains. She didn't use the term "refugee," but that's what he was, a refugee running for his life.

As far as we were concerned, Nini was the queen of the universe with her auburn, glowy hair, almond eyes, and high cheekbones, an Indigenous woman from the cradle of civilization. Nini was becoming my best friend, another rebel loudmouth finding her way as a feminist woman and a fellow border crosser.

Then there was Tammis, who was white and raised in privilege in the private schools of Connecticut with a banker father. Yet she too was a rebel, a filmmaker, an artist, and someone who defined bohemian life. Tammis, who was two years older than most of my friends, showed us all how to do it. She had her own apartment in a tenement building with thrifted furniture and a futon on the floor and her black-and-white photographs on all the walls.

The beginning of college reminded me of when I moved into private high school as once again I felt a giddy desire to take advantage of everything I possibly could. When would I ever have this chance again? My freshman year I signed up for six classes, including a senior-level economics class studying Marxist political theory. Of course, I bit off a little more than

I could chew and ended up having to drop that class and take another one pass/fail.

I auditioned for a dance troupe, but I had become too scared to audition for theater after my last experience in Chicago auditioning for the city's first Latino theater company. That director had told me he didn't "get" me. He said I wasn't Mexican enough. I wasn't white enough. I wasn't tall enough or short enough or street enough or sophisticated enough. He told me he didn't see me in the world of theater or Hollywood acting. And I let this guy I'd never met before tell me who I was. It was something I wouldn't do again.

Instead of acting, I decided to study more dance, try Afro Cuban dance, which is much harder than it looks, and choreograph performances on campus. Then there was the student-run radio station WKCR. It was another way to be visible and invisible at the same time—visible through my voice, but behind a microphone on the airwaves.

I also became active with multiple organizing groups, including the Chicano caucus, as it was known at the time. Then I joined Alianza Latino Americana, which was more Caribbean and Puerto Rican. I was living among refugees from Argentina, Chile, and Colombia, and now I was meeting more people from El Salvador and Guatemala. I was hearing about US military intervention in Central America. There were increasing protests and sometimes it felt like 1968 and Vietnam all over again. In 1981 it was happening in Central America in places I'd never been to, never seen. But as a borderless young Latina, I knew those places were a part of me too. In those groups, we demanded the US government do better in countries that were connected to my Latina roots, where Spanish was spoken, where there were Indigenous people, Black people, poor people, women, and children who needed and wanted to be seen and not abused.

My activism was spurred on by being at a women's college. I thrived on being in a community supported by women. I loved being challenged and put into highly competitive situations. Barnard sat across the street from Columbia University, and though the two colleges remained separate, they shared resources and Barnard students like me were allowed to take courses at Columbia. I often found myself in classes with lots of smart (or so they said) men and forced my hand up in the air to ask a question. I wanted them to see me. *Yes, I'm right here in front of you.*

That skill of pushing my arm up, forcing myself to ask the professor a question even though I was trembling inside with the butterflies and everything, was the same impulse that had pushed me onto the stage as an actress. It was the voice that said, *Go ahead and write that essay, apply to Barnard, go ahead and make that audition.* It was the voice that said, *Go to the other side—you have to, your family didn't leave everything behind for you not to.* The sacrifices my parents made for me were a heavy load to carry, but they also motivated me to take advantage of everything. *This education was not given to you. You're not rich like other kids so take advantage and be a radical and find your path.*

My first year in college was by no means the year that I

figured out where my life was headed. But I learned some seminal lessons about being open to difference and change, exploring your identity, and being kind and respectful to others. I learned to find myself in people I never expected to see myself in: a woman from Iran, a working class white guy from Massachusetts, an Argentinian from New Jersey, and so many others I met in New York. I was connecting with people who on the surface had nothing in common with me. And yet here we were sharing this tight space, the streets and small apartments of upper Manhattan, the bodegas and subways, offering our stories to one another, and finding joy in the simple experience of living together with all of our differences.

CHAPTER 18

Embracing My Latina-ness

The way I saw it, college was about doing the intellectual work of understanding who you are. I was proud of the young woman I had been in high school, who was a badass, doing what she wanted when she wanted, whether it was acting on the stage, getting boyfriends, studying and scoring good grades, working hard, making money, or traveling on her own (all while battling imposter syndrome and morning pukes). And now I was watching that young woman develop into a more secure, though still finding her footing, version of herself. My hair became a barometer of my wildness. It kept getting longer, thicker, curlier. It defined who I wanted to be: someone who was not going to fit into anyone's constricting little box.

I was learning about and getting inspired by Mexican women who were bohemian artists, academics, and activists—so different from my cousins, who made me feel like to be a real Mexican woman I needed to dress up like a doll. These were the women of resistance, the women who protested the 1968 Olympics in Mexico City and were shot down by the Mexican Armed Forces, as described by journalist Elena Poniatowska in her groundbreaking book *La Noche de Tlatelolco*. They were the women artists I had been with through many late nights in Mexico City, who had shared their journeys and escapades. It was my cousin who owned her Indigenous self and had moved to Oaxaca to embrace her heritage as an anthropologist. These women were becoming my role models.

But in New York City, I quickly realized my identity as a Mexican woman, which I was still working so hard to cultivate and understand, was of little importance to anyone. It was like, *Yeah, no one really cares that you're Mexican. There are no Mexicans here.* The Day of the Dead, tortillas, salsa picante, diez-y-seis de septiembre, festival de la raza—none of those things existed in New York at that time.

This forced me to acknowledge my own personal geography and how it had shaped me. I wasn't just a Mexican woman, but a Mexican woman born in Mexico City who grew up in Hyde Park on the South Side of Chicago in the Midwest and spent her weekends in El Barrio Mexicano. And now I was a Mexican living in New York City near Spanish Harlem where mostly Puerto Ricans lived. How did I fit into all this geography? How did I fit in politically? To answer this question, I had to think about my identity in a more radical way. I had to go to the root.

At Barnard I heard people talk about how America extended from Canada all the way down to Tierra del Fuego at the tip of South America. This was a geographical revelation. None of this had been taught to me in high school. Mexico was next to the United States, but the rest of Latin America was unclear and ill-defined in my mind. In high school, we'd been taught that places in the south weren't that important while, of course, we studied European maps and knew the capitals of each country there.

On campus I kept on meeting people from everywhere, which meant I had to come to terms with how much I didn't know. I met a woman from the Dominican Republic and I'm ashamed to admit this, but I asked her, "Where is that?" I had no idea. I had never met anyone from the Dominican Republic in Chicago.

Altagracia Dilone was my first Afro Latina friend and she was proud of her African roots. Altagracia was a true Dominican so she didn't hide how disgusted she was that I didn't know where the Dominican Republic was. But over the months I proved myself and she became a dear friend. She was another role model and a groundbreaker doing things in her own way with her own style. There was no one else who looked like her on campus and she couldn't have cared less. Her hair was down to her waist and it was the biggest part of her slim body, a mass of tight waves that you could see from afar that shouted, *I am a proud Black woman.*

I met Chilean and Argentinian refugees who had been relocated from their homes in South America to the Upper West Side in Manhattan. Over the years I had heard stories about Argentina and Chile from my parents' conversations. I had watched on television as General Augusto Pinochet and his military overthrew Chile's progressive civilian government on September 11, 1973. Here in New York, years later, were the people whose lives had been uprooted by those events. They were refugees living in our midst who spoke a different kind of Spanish, one that I had to strain to understand.

Puerto Ricans were everywhere in New York City, and there was a story behind their arrival in the US, too. Their beautiful island became booty in the Spanish American War. American soldiers invaded Puerto Rico, which had been colonized by Spain centuries before, and in 1898, as the war ended, Spain agreed to "give" the island to the US under the Treaty of Paris. Puerto Rico became a US territory. In 1917, Puerto Ricans were granted US citizenship, making it easier for them to migrate north for job opportunities, which many began doing in increasing numbers after 1945 when they were recruited by companies and the US government. Still, Puerto Rico remains a colonial possession of the United States to this day.

At that time, Puerto Ricans were massively recruited to come to New York because the city needed a new source of cheap factory labor. Thousands of Puerto Rican families were ripped apart and Puerto Ricans became the first massive Latino population in New York City. Through decades of activism, Puerto Ricans had built up an influence in New York City that Mexicans in Chicago were only just starting to grab hold of. The Young Lords were an activist group that started in Chicago, but their New York City chapter was the one that made headlines. They fought against racism, fed the hungry, provided community health care, and rallied for Puerto Rican independence in a coalition that welcomed all colonized and marginalized people to join them.

Puerto Rican culture was intertwined into many different parts of the city. There were the deep, alluring, and evocative sounds of salsa music blasting from open windows below 110th Street and on boom boxes on Broadway. Nuyorican Poets (a New York Puerto Rican is a Nuyorican) were performing on the Lower East Side, spitting poetry verses in vacant lots or in an East Village living room salon where audiences gathered, which eventually became the famed Nuyorican Poets Cafe. I met Cubans who called themselves revolutionaries and Nuyorican artists like Adál, Pedro Pietri, and Miguel Algarin.

I took the idea of New York City being my college campus seriously, and I was on the subway heading off campus most weekends. I was in lofts on the dark streets of Chelsea at political dance parties, and on the Lower East Side and in the South Bronx I was going to community theater, galleries, and speakeasies where I met Latinos and Latinas from everywhere.

These new friends from different communities were my mentors, the people I looked up to, and their friendship was their way of saying, *We want to give this young woman a sense of power. We want to give her a sense of recognition so that she realizes her own power. We're going to reflect our own influence back on her.* As a young Latina in the Ivy League, I was a rare bird. There were not that many of us, maybe a few dozen. They saw a light in me that I couldn't see yet, and because they believed in me, I began to believe in myself.

I began to see myself in relation to other Latin peoples as a Pan-Latin Americanist. Although my nationality was Mexican, I was also part of an entire continent. I was part of a Latino and Latina movement that connected Chicanos and Chicanas in Los Angeles to the Brown Berets in Texas and *Sin Fronteras* magazine in Chicago and extended out to Puerto Ricans, Dominicans, Cubans, and so many others in New York and beyond.

Back home in Chicago after my first year of college, I had fresh notions of how I wanted to spend my summer. I did not want to go back to being a waitress. Though I still needed to make money to support myself through the next school year, I had a strong desire to make a difference. Luckily, I found a way to do both. Because of people like my brother and Beatriz and other young activists who saw me as a young Latina and budding activist, the organizers at Casa Aztlán in El Barrio gave me a job running part of their summer youth program.

Casa Aztlán was an art center named after the ancestral lands of the Aztecs. Legend has it that all Mexicans came from a place called Aztlán, though historians still debate its exact location, possibly part of what is now the Southwest United States. What we do know is that after Mexico lost the Mexican-American War in 1848, US leaders forced the Mexican government to sign the Treaty of Guadalupe Hidalgo and give away more than half its land to the United States government. The borders of what we call Mexico have moved many times.

My job at Casa Aztlán was to create and run a summer program for kindergartners. I was a nineteen-year-old who was somehow now responsible for overseeing about forty-five children under the age of seven. Four high school students were assigned to be my employees and help coordinate the various activities. I'd never done anything like this before so the job was a bit daunting, but everyone at Casa Aztlán believed I could do it. I was like, *Okay, well, if they believe I can do it, I guess I've got to do this.* They had already taken care of enrolling students, but I was in charge and the kids would be with me from nine in the morning until one in the afternoon.

The little kids ended up being a cinch. My high school employees were the ones who posed the biggest challenge. On the first day of the program, a typical Chicago summer day with temperatures in the nineties, I had the kids sit in a circle in the church gymnasium. There was no one else to look to for help because I was the boss. I felt the same kind of nervous energy I'd experienced right before jumping on stage for a theater production. *Well, here we go*, I told myself. *Do the best you can.*

The morning activities went by in a blur and I felt lucky to have four student workers who could each take on a group of eight to ten kids. Once the last little kid was picked up by their family around one p.m., I spent the rest of the afternoon talking to the student workers about what I expected of them. They were fourteen and fifteen years old and in the proving-themselves-to-everyone phase. There was Babyface, who was Puerto Rican with a budding goatee; Mario, who the kids teased because he had been in Chicago less than a year and hardly spoke English; Toughie, with a broken front tooth and an angry look in his eyes; and Teresa, who had big dreams of becoming a working professional as well as a big crush on Babyface.

I was trying to set the tone for how we were going to work together. I told them that I needed them to take this job seriously and that they were role models the kids were going to be looking up to. By treating me as an equal, Beatriz and others had shown me my own power and how I, too, could lead; I was trying to do the same for my student workers by handing down leadership responsibilities to them.

The problem was, these kids had a built-in distrust of someone like me who wasn't from their neighborhood, who spoke this perfect English, and who in their eyes looked like a rich girl. The fact that I lived in multiple different realities and that I was this border crosser—we didn't yet have the term "code switch" to describe how people like me shift between English and Spanish or from Hyde Park to El Barrio—was staring me in the face. In all the conversations around my identity, the one thing I hadn't grappled with yet was my own privilege.

I didn't see myself as someone who was entitled or came from a wealthy family. I grew up in an immigrant family and was raised by a Mexican father who was very controlling when it came to money. He lived in a perpetual state of "never enough," and, by extension, so did we.

We didn't do the things some of my private high school friends could afford, like annual ski trips to Aspen or family vacations to Europe. I did not consider myself part of the upper class because I knew people who had a lot more money than my family. They lived in three-story houses on individual plots of land while we lived in an apartment with families above and below us. Many of my high school and college class-mates' families even had second homes in places like Michigan City, Colorado, and Florida.

Any money I had was money I earned by working. When I waitressed, I would gather my tips at the end of the night and put them away in an envelope to be saved. Freshman year at Barnard I worked at the library, did odd jobs around campus, and babysat. So I did not see myself as someone who was financially privileged.

But to Babyface, Teresa, Mario, and Toughie, I was a privileged girl from the South Side, an outsider. They were super tough because gangs were a daily reality in El Barrio and they had to stay alert to protect themselves—and that meant distrusting strangers. They needed me to know that while I might be proud of being Mexican, they were survivors. They were the ones who really knew how things ran around here.

Toughie was the outspoken one of the group.

"Excuse me, Miss Maria, but what do you know about living out? You don't be living here. Don't play like that," he said.

"That's true, but I've been coming here to Pilsen since I was a kid. I love this place and I respect it and I want the best for everyone here," I responded.

"That sounds like some white girl stuff."

"Come on. That's low," I said, hurt.

"I don't care. I just wanna get paid." Toughie shrugged.

"Well, to do that, you have to show up and respect me and the job."

"You gotta respect me first," he said.

I stopped. I walked up to him and looked in his eyes and said, "Te respeto. A ti y a tu familia."

"I don't speak Spanish," he said. His eyebrows were pulling in and he was looking like he was going to step to me.

I said very quickly, "My bad, Toughie, I'm sorry. I said I do respect you and your family. I respect you." He pulled back. It was better but not over. This was going to require hard work on my end.

I walked into work the next morning at eight-thirty a.m. and heard the song of the summer, Queen's "Another One Bites the Dust," blasting from a boombox at full volume. My four students were sitting around rolling joints. They had brought pot into our workplace. I had to step to them and speak from my heart.

I told them how much I believed in them. I said I didn't care if they smoked pot outside of work, but they couldn't be doing that here because if they got caught with pot, especially while they were with the little kids, the entire summer program and Casa Aztlán would go under. I knew they didn't want that to happen because they loved their community. I said, "I know and trust that you guys won't do this again."

They stepped to me and asked me again why they should respect me if I wasn't from Pilsen. I affirmed their questioning of me. I told them I would do the same if I was them. But I asked them to give me a shot, too. I recognized they had power here and I was humbly asking for a chance to prove myself and show them my respect for them and for Pilsen. I said we may not like each other, but either way we were going to be together the entire summer.

I asked if they would show me their Pilsen and I told them which tortilleria I used, which grocery stores my family shopped at, and the carnicero I knew by name. "Even though I don't live here, it doesn't mean I'm not a part of this community or that my paesanos don't have a right to better opportunities and a better education."

Though the kids had been angry at first, after I said my piece, they were dumbfounded that I had taken the time to explain myself to them. They were used to being shut down. Their reaction was like, *Wow, this lady spent all this time talking to us like we matter.*

That moment of confrontation ended with mutual respect, and after that day, the five of us became inseparable. They would bring food from home to share with me. I would buy them coffee and donuts. One weekend I took the four of them on a field trip to the Art Institute of Chicago, which they had never visited. We became a family. I learned to see people and meet them where they are and treat them with respect. I wanted to be their Beatriz.

At the end of the summer, the community was planning to host a celebration called Festival del Sol. My student workers and I had agreed that we would go together. However, on the day of the festival Babyface told me he couldn't go because he was in the Latin Kings gang and the festival was being held on enemy territory. He might get shot just for being there. In the 1980s, gangs were common in Chicago. The city itself has a long history of organized crime. Babyface was only fifteen and wanted out of the gang—he and Teresa had plans to make it out of El Barrio together—but it wasn't that simple.

"You're coming," I said. "I'm going to stand in front of you so no one will see you or shoot at you." Babyface came to the festival and I stood in front of him the whole time.

This Barrio Mexicano was *my* Barrio Mexicano. Now I knew the people who lived in the neighborhood and had visited their homes. There wasn't a lot of food in my students' households. Their parents were rarely home because they had to work all the time. The poverty they experienced was real and also complicated. There was no easy answer.

Every day that summer I commuted to Pilsen by catching the bus from our apartment in Hyde Park, then transferred to the elevated train and got off at 18th Street, and walked five blocks north. Something about seeing my privilege every day made me begin to understand how thankful I was for everything I did have. By acknowledging my privilege and my power as one of the few Latinas from the city of Chicago going to an Ivy League school in the Big Apple, I had to own my power and turn it into a sense of responsibility. *How can I help?* That was my purpose and reason for returning to El Barrio. And it was a question that would stay with me when I returned to school in the fall.

CHAPTER 19

Finding My Voice on the Airwaves

I arrived back in New York in September with a renewed sense of purpose, and brought the lessons and experiences from El Barrio with me. Dorm life wasn't for me, so I had decided to move off campus into a tenement apartment building with my friend Tammis. Even though she came from a privileged background as a young white woman from Connecticut, she was the one in our friend group, along with me, who had chosen to live among Dominicans and Puerto Ricans in a neighborhood that most Ivy League students and their parents considered "dangerous." It was the Upper West Side, for god's sake, and only eight blocks away from campus.

Everybody in our neighborhood was Brown or Black and spoke Spanish. I understood everything that was being said and most of the time people were just talking about everyday things. To me, Spanish Harlem was the best of all the worlds coming together, like Hyde Park and Pilsen all in one.

I fell in love with my new home immediately. The building was old and funky and looked like it was straight out of
West Side Story. Our apartment was a fifth-floor walk-up,
meaning there was no elevator, only stairs, and we had to walk
all the way up no matter how tired we were, no matter how
many heavy grocery bags we were carrying. Inside, the creaky,
uneven wooden floors hadn't been sanded in years. You could
never walk barefoot for fear of getting a splinter the size of a
worm. We were in a constant battle with cockroaches, and this
was my first experience with these nasty little survivors that are
everywhere in New York City no matter what you do.

Tammis, who was an aspiring filmmaker and photographer,
had two small rooms, one to sleep in and the other to work on
her projects. I also had two small rooms. The apartment was
a tenement, which meant that each apartment was designed
with many rooms for many people to sleep in as new migrants
to the city. My rooms overlooked the fire escape. Through the
open windows I could hear the rat-tat-tat-tat-tat of Dominican
Spanish, sometimes being spoken in loud arguments, angry
screaming matches between a couple. The smell of habichuelas,
as they're called in the Dominican Republic (frijoles to me), and
adobo cooking on our neighbors' stoves wafted into our apartment on the regular. My parents knew that I had moved off
campus and liked that I was saving money by doing so, since
they were helping me with the rent. My share was one hundred
thirty-five dollars a month. I earned about twenty-five dollars
per babysitting gig, so it took me six nights of babysitting to earn
enough money to cover rent each month.

I was coming into my own as an independent woman and becoming a New York version of Beatriz. I decorated my rooms with Mexican textiles from Oaxaca and photographs I had taken of my friends and coworkers in Pilsen. I was dabbling in photography to see if maybe photojournalism was for me. Every day when I woke up I'd look around my tidy bedroom decorated with things that connected me to my ancestral Mexican roots and feel joy.

I was not a young Mexican woman living in the Mexican neighborhood in Chicago. I was a Latina immigrant living in a mixed Latino neighborhood, among all different kinds of Spanish speakers: Dominicans, Puerto Ricans, Cubans, Argentinians, Chileans, Colombians, and, increasingly, Central Americans.

After my summer in Pilsen, reintegrating into campus life was jarring at first. I still had a vivid picture in my mind of protecting Babyface from getting shot by a rival gang at the Festival del Sol. My friends in New York didn't understand what I was talking about. Poverty and gang violence were the furthest thing from their minds and experiences. Cecilia thought what I'd done was cool, but she also had no clue what it was really like. I realized that this feeling of disconnect was the way it was going to be. There were parts of myself that lived in different geographic spaces. I had to know and love the border crosser in me now that I was living between two different cities, two different realities, two different experiences of being a Latina in the United States.

Sophomore year I registered for classes that focused more

on Latin American studies and women's studies so that I could explore my feminist identity. One day, not too far into the academic year, I got a phone call from Carlos and José Luiz at WKCR, the Columbia University radio station.

The guys hadn't forgotten about me, and somehow they'd tracked me down. We didn't have email, cell phones, or even voicemail back then. If someone called you, you had to be home to actually answer the phone. They called me and I went in to meet with them in one of the common spaces at Ferris Booth Hall, the building where the radio station and student organizations were housed. (FBH has since been rebuilt and, hopefully, thoroughly cleaned, but the place was historic because many of the meetings for the Columbia 1968 protests took place in that sacred space.)

As I was sitting on an old, gross couch and listening to these two adorable Latino music nerds talk about their radio show, it slowly dawned on me that they were asking me to take over their Wednesday night salsa music slot.

What was going on here? I was hardly a Latin music aficionado and knew nothing about salsa. I had ten records from La Nueva Canción and had started listening to protest music by musicians like Victor Jara and Silvio Rodriguez. But I didn't know where to get more records in New York and I had never been a radio disc jockey before. I was a second-year college student with no experience. How could they ask this of me? My face must have given away the utter shock and surprise I was feeling. I was petrified and really feeling like an imposter, even with my own people.

"Look, the reason why we're doing this is because we

don't really have a choice," one of them finally said. "We've lost members. People have become less politicized over the last decade. They don't realize the political commitment and statement that these radio programs make on the campus and in the city. If we don't fill the time slot, we'll lose it—and you know how hard previous students fought to get these slots in the first place. I mean, they fought for our voices to be heard. We can't just walk away. There is no one else who can do this except you."

"But all I have is ten records," I said.

"Ten records is more than zero. We'll help you figure this out. We'll talk to record companies and get them to start sending music to you. But you have to do this for the people."

Carlos and José Luiz didn't use the word "la raza," but I knew that was what they meant. They looked at me as an equal and believed I could do anything, though I wasn't sure of that at all. They also didn't give me a chance to say no. I had to believe what they were saying was true: that because they believed in me, I could do this. The power you have when you believe in someone else and the power you feel when someone believes in you more than you believe in yourself, can be world-changing.

Two weeks later I was spending all my hours in the live studio booth with the other DJs and watching everything they did: how they played the music, gently laying down the needle on the LPs; how they spoke into the microphone, at a short distance so as not to pop the Ps; which buttons they had to push to keep things running smoothly—so many buttons! I had to learn how to do this all by myself. They would be there the first few shows, but then I was on my own.

The first night I went on the air, my voice was trembling. So were my hands, which made it very difficult to put the needle down on the record without it jumping around. The day before the show, I wrote out a list of every single song I planned to play so that I would have all my records in order. I wanted to know exactly which album to put on next. I welcomed listeners, introduced myself by my first name only, and told them the name of the show was *Nueva Canción y Demás*. After each song, I told people what they had listened to and the names of the musicians on the album. I sounded like one of those classical music DJs I had grown up listening to on WFMT in Chicago—removed and almost robotic, though I did my best to make my voice gentle and welcoming.

That's how it went in the beginning until the work began to feel more routine. I saw how the other DJs at the station were having fun at the job. They weren't wracked with insecurity like I was, though maybe I felt that way because there were so few women on the air. But now that I knew the buttons, now that my hand wasn't shaking when I was putting the needle on the album, now that I could read what was in front of me without my voice trembling, I realized I needed to be me. The seeds I had planted were taking root and giving me a tender base from which to find my own expression.

Within a couple of months, Cecilia was joining me for my weekly Wednesday night slot from ten p.m. to one a.m. so that I wouldn't have to walk home at that hour by myself. Cecilia, after one year of college, was even more radical than I was. One night after the show she said, "You know, we really shouldn't be doing the show in English. English is the language of colonizers. We should be speaking in Spanish, even though Spanish is also a language of colonizers, but at least it's ours."

By this point in my life, English had become my dominant language, and my Spanish was accented and rusty. So I said to her, "Our Spanish is nowhere near good enough."

"We can do fine. And it's a way for us to make a statement about the Spanish language being important."

A movement to declare English the official language of the United States had been gaining steam in recent years, starting with an anti-bilingual ordinance in Dade County, Florida, in 1980. One year later Virginia declared English as its official language. We could take a stand and indicate our position as proud Spanish speakers by doing our show in Spanish on the Columbia University radio station.

So we did. And it did make a statement, but not the one we expected. People called us up and said, "What's the matter with your Spanish? You all need to speak better Spanish." It was hard to hear, but we took the criticism in stride. The next week on the show we addressed the issue head on.

"We know that a lot of listeners have a problem with the way we speak Spanish because it's not perfect. We're college students doing this with love and we're trying to do better. We want to reclaim our language, so please correct us. We'll take your feedback." That softened them on the other end of the line, hearing that we were trying. Estabamos tratando!

Every couple of months the Latin music department, including the guys who DJed the Monday and Friday night slots, would meet with us at Ferris Booth Hall. Carlos and José Luiz would hug me and tell me how proud they were of me. I was officially a member of the WKCR community. They gave me the capacity to see my own power. "People are listening. They like what you're doing. It's never been done before. Keep doing it," they said.

Nueva Canción y Demás took over a time slot that had originally been dedicated to salsa, a type of music that comes from Cuban and Puerto Rican traditions. Gradually I came to realize that salsa was deeply political. The people of Puerto Rico were doing their best to survive as one of the last American colonies. Even flying the Puerto Rican flag, which the US government had banned on the island when they first took over, was political. Simply playing the music of this island with its socialist Afro-Cuban roots was a political statement.

Cecilia and I were just as political as our predecessors, but with a different style. Instead of exclusively salsa, we played music from Chile, Argentina, Nicaragua, and Mexico, as well as protest music from Cuba and Puerto Rico. The show's opening song became "A Desalambrar!" from Expresion Joven, an Afro-Dominican activist group of musicians. "A desalambrar" means to tear down the fences, the ones that separate the poor from everybody else in the Dominican Republic and across the world. Latino New Yorkers who listened to WKCR got the vibe, la vibra, of the show because it breathed life into the idea of Latinidad and Pan-Latin American solidarity.

With the privilege of hosting *Nueva Canción y Demás* also came responsibility. WKCR was transmitted on the radio waves to people as far away as ninety miles. We were one of the most listened-to noncommercial radio stations in the city. We had clout and visibility. Some of the first mail I received was from people in prison in Upstate New York. Our incarcerated brothers and sisters were listening to *Nueva Canción y Demás* and writing us letters every month. I had to process the power of radio and the power of my own voice on it.

Of course, not everyone loved us. There were plenty of people who did not like what we were doing, the way we sounded, or that Cecilia had an Argentinian accent, which many perceived to be a symbol of absolute whiteness and privilege (and Cecilia had both). But we were two young women in the Ivy League who were deeply committed to creating a space for all kinds of Latin music: Puerto Rican, Mexican, Argentinian, Dominican, Cuban, Colombian. It was one big community and we had to support one another. It was like Simón Bolívar's dream of a unified Latin America happening right here in northern Manhattan.

Little by little, we started to get phone calls from people saying, *Thank you for what you're doing. Your music choices are beautiful. Thank you for playing the music of Mercedes Sosa. Thank you for playing the music of Pablo Milanés. Thank you for playing the music of Quilapayún and Inti-Illimani. Thank you for playing Indigenous rhythms.*

That winter break, Cecilia joined me and my parents on our family's yearly trip. This time, instead of driving, we flew and spent a few days at a beach spot in Manzanillo before moving on to Mexico City. Cecilia was getting to know the place where I was born and had spent so much of my youth. I took her to the pyramid city at Teotihuacan and to Librería Gandhi where we bought every album of political and folklore music we could possibly find. WKCR had given us a budget to bring back records for our show. We spent some of our own money, too.

That trip with Cecilia cemented my friendship with her. We had traveled together to my homeland. She had met my parents, mis tios y tias, and my cousins, several of whom were completely enamored with her. She had seen my roots. Now we truly were hermanas.

Underneath the cool new music we were discovering and playing on the radio was something more serious. Artists had created this music in response to events taking place in Latin America. This was musica de protesta, musica de demanda, music with a message, though it was also about partying and life and hope.

In 1979, the Sandinistas had overthrown the brutal dictator Anastasio Somoza Debayle and sparked the Nicaraguan Revolution. I'd heard about Nicaragua as a little girl because of a devastating earthquake that struck the country in 1972. My parents had a friend there they wanted to help. He told them stories of how their dictator president took the blood that had been donated for the injured in his country, and instead of giving it to his people, he turned around and sold it on the international market. Now, finally liberated from Somoza, the new leftist government there was asking for international volunteers to help in a massive national literacy program to teach people in Nicaragua, the most illiterate country in the Western Hemisphere, how to read.

El Salvador, right next to Nicaragua, was ruled by a government that massacred its own people; soldiers there killed thirty thousand Indigenous people in 1932 for speaking out against government oppression. Inspired by the way the people in Nicaragua had come together to topple a cruel and unjust leader, Salvadorans soon took up arms and became guerilla fighters in the streets in 1979.

Cecilia kept saying there was no way we could keep playing protest music without talking about the politics behind the music. *Nueva Canción y Demás* quickly became a place for this kind of dialogue. Every Wednesday night, organizers from political organizations in New York City and activists from all over Latin America came on the show to talk about their work. For example, we invited organizers from the Bronx who were protesting the making of the movie *Fort Apache, The Bronx*, which depicted Puerto Ricans stereotypically as people addicted to heroin; they asked the community to bang on pots and pans during filming, which made it nearly impossible to finish shooting any scenes. We talked to Puerto Rican activists who were fighting for independence. The show became more radical at every turn.

Listeners began to realize that we were the place to go if you wanted to know what was going on with Colombian activists on the left or Salvadoran women revolutionaries or

Mexican folklore performers coming to Lincoln Center. People would stay up late to listen to us and call in to say, *Next week so-and-so is visiting from this organization.* Or, *There's this protest happening. Can we come and talk about it on the air?* We'd say "sure" and that's how it happened. La voz se corrio.

One night, a year into the show, I got a phone call from a stranger who told me he worked at National Public Radio (NPR). He said, "You know, you really should consider a career in radio. You have an amazing voice."

I remember laughing at him and saying, "That's so funny. Why would you think that?"

"You don't hear it, but you have a voice for radio." And he added, "You should really think seriously about doing this with your life."

I might not have fully believed in my voice yet, so I had to hear those words from someone on the outside, but at least I listened.

CHAPTER 20

Travels with Jorge

Mom and Dad had planted seeds of curiosity in all four of their children and now each of us was on a journey to understanding our identities. My sister, Bertha Elena, had started her college experience in Mexico City thinking she would become an anthropologist, and then decided to become a special education teacher for preschool children who were autistic or hearing impaired. My brother Raúl was doing research in Oaxaca and continuing his activism in electoral politics and grassroots organizing, only now in Berkeley, Oaxaca, and in the pueblos in the mountains.

My brother Jorge, the third child, had decided to differentiate himself by learning to speak Portuguese. He signed up for a six-month study program in Rio de Janeiro, Brazil. By the end of my sophomore year, I had saved a couple of thousand dollars from my multiple odd jobs—projectionist for an art history class, waitress, student worker reshelving library books, receptionist at the YMCA, babysitter—to meet Jorge after his language courses ended and join him on his travels in South America for the summer.

Although Brazil was a part of Latin America, it seemed very foreign to me. I knew they didn't speak Spanish there, but that was about it. Why didn't our fancy private high school teach us anything about this massive country and its cultural influence? Brazil is geographically larger than the US! Instead of back-packing through Europe, like many of our college friends were doing, we headed south to Brazil, Paraguay, Argentina, Bolivia, and wherever the wind blew us al sur.

The trip would be an opportunity to learn some Portuguese, improve my Spanish, and learn about South America firsthand through my own adventures—all things I couldn't do sitting in a classroom at Barnard. It would also enable me to collect more music, which WKCR had given me a small budget for. Before flying down to Brazil, I splurged and bought myself a cutting-edge Sony Walkman radio/cassette player. I figured cassettes would be easier to carry home in my backpack.

Making plans for after graduation was the furthest thing from my mind. Between DJing at WKCR every week, waking up early to study for my classes, learning taekwondo, and working multiple jobs (so Mexican-y, so immigrant-y), all I'd focused on was work for the past year. Now that I was in Brazil and had enough money to keep me going for a few months, I didn't have to worry about working at all. Instead, I focused on being present in the moment, which was easy, I was learning, when you have nothing to do every day except live.

This four-month period of nonstop traveling was one of the most beautiful times in my life. I felt unrestricted and free in every sense of the word. I was meeting people from the countries I was traveling through, which were varied and complex and complicated, as well as people from all over the world. It was one of the longest stretches in my life when I did not have any interactions with Americans. The only Americans I came across were Mormons proselytizing in Cusco, Peru. They stood out in their white button-down shirts and black name tags, holding Bibles in their hands as they walked among the Indigenous Inca people in the mountains and the Plaza Central.

So much of life in the United States was about rushing to get from Point A to Point B, like being in a competitive race to get somewhere first though you're not even sure where that somewhere is or why you're going there. In South America, I met people who worked six months out of the year as restaurant servers and spent the rest of the year traveling to places where they could live on twenty dollars a day. Still, that was more money than a lot of young people had. I was seeing privilege in the face of need.

Brazil was light and fresh. It smelled of citrus and gardenias, of beaches and saltwater and waves. There is one song that captures the feeling of being there and brings me back every time—"Lua de São Jorge" by Caetano Veloso. Everything there felt different. Maybe it was because Brazil is on the other side of the Earth in the Southern Hemisphere. Even the water gets sucked down the toilet bowl in the opposite direction. I know this because I watched, fascinated, after every flush.

Rio de Janeiro was a lush tropical city by the ocean, built on top of rocky hills, nothing like the concrete jungle of New York. The red of the hibiscus flowers was so vibrant it looked as if they was on fire. The mangoes being sold by vendors on every street corner were so ripe and ready to eat you could smell them from half a block away. The smiles were bigger. The bathing suits were tinier.

But there was another part of Rio that could be seen everywhere: the favelas. This gorgeous place, one of the seven natural wonders of the world, also had one of the most horrific poverty rates on the planet. The city of glamorous living was surrounded by hills filled with people living in cardboard shantytowns. If they were lucky, they lived in a cement structure with a sink, but for many that wasn't a possibility. When it rained, the people in the favelas cried. The mud would stream down the unpaved streets and take everything with it: the garbage, their pet cats, or even their houses.

The world was filled with contradictions and beauty was always tempered. My eyes were open to it all. Jorge, who now spoke Portuguese fluently and had gained some understanding of the place after six months, framed it this way: "Rio is about the image that is presented on the outside," he told me. There were so many beautiful apartment buildings with grand entrances that lined the avenues of upscale neighborhoods, but when you went inside, the apartments were small, dark, and old. That helped me to understand a little bit more about Rio.

Next we traveled to Southern Brazil where we came upon a community of Brazilians who were of German descent. They had blond hair and blue eyes and lived in extreme poverty. That was shocking to me—to see white people speaking Portuguese and living in total squalor. Being able to have my own biases deconstructed right before my eyes was humbling and powerful.

At the time, Brazil was being ruled by a military dictatorship. Dictatorships were something I had only read about in books, that happened in other countries. For the first time in my life, I got to witness one myself. My brother had become friends with many young activists from the Partido de Trabajadores, or PT, a group that was outlawed by the Brazilian government. I met some of these labor activists and they told me they were afraid for their lives. They were human beings who wanted justice for other human beings, but fighting for that in a military dictatorship meant they had to put their lives on the line. I met people prepared to go to prison or die for what they believed.

When we continued west and crossed the border into Paraguay, we came face-to-face with a whole new level of government control. To enter the country, we had to surrender our passports to government officials at the border. After twenty-four hours they sent the passports on to Asunción, the capital, or wherever our destination was, and we'd have to pick them up there.

Paraguay was ruled by the dictator Alfredo Stroessner, the son of Bavarian immigrants, who had been in power for more than thirty years. There were very few white people in Paraguay. As our bus passed through the countryside, we saw only

Indigenous people. The capital city was much more mixed than the countryside had been, but there was a massive Indigenous population there too. Guaraní, the local Indigenous language, is still spoken everywhere in Paraguay.

Jorge and I found a place to stay at a youth hostel in downtown Asunción, based on the recommendations of a four-inch-thick guidebook we carried around with us. I began to make friends right away. Unlike Brazil, where you saw people partying on the streets of Rio, Asunción was a serious place. There, in the interior of South America, it was colder and darker. People were more reserved.

In Brazil, I had met Black people who spoke Portuguese and white people who lived in poverty. In Paraguay, I saw how a dictatorship run by a white man oppressed the majority population of Indigenous people and stripped them of any power. It was a scary place, and I was relieved when we left. But it was fascinating to see the white people speak the Guaraní language with pride.

Jorge and I traveled to Argentina next and made our way, on rickety buses and on foot, through the purple mountains of La Cordillera. These were the same mountains that Mercedes Sosa and Atahualpa Yupanqui sang about, where Cecilia traced her roots back to. Since the seasons are reversed in the Southern Hemisphere—when it's summer in North America, it's winter in South America—it was chilly, especially in the mountains. The smell of wood burning from every house's chimney filled the air.

People seemed to like the fact that we were a brother and sister traveling together with the blessing of our parents. It prompted a certain level of tenderness. We would meet people on the street, often selling something, and we'd start talking—and before we knew it, they were inviting us to their home.

"De donde son ustedes?" they would ask us. And the first thing out of our mouths was, "Nosotros somos Mexicanos pero vivimos en los Estados Unidos." *We're Mexican but we live in the United States.* Their reaction was like, *Wow, Mexicans.* I think they were pleasantly surprised, because so few Mexicans traveled to this part of the world. You had to have a certain amount of wealth to be able to travel like that. Even if it only cost fifteen dollars a day to survive, for the people who lived in the countries we visited, fifteen dollars might feel more like a hundred dollars. They didn't always have fifteen dollars to spend and often had to get by on much less. Being able to spend that kind of money every day was a luxury.

In Salta, a family asked us to join them to make empanadas. They were perhaps the most delicious empanadas I've ever eaten in my life. I'll always be searching for the empanada that takes me back to that moment. The crust was warm but not hot, crispy on the outside only, and the inside crust almost melted into the seasoned ground beef with raisins and cumin. I have yet to find it all these decades later.

The humility of these people, their capacity to open their hearts and share what little they had with us, was striking. They told us their family stories and asked questions to learn about us, these Mexican kids from New York and Chicago. It was a mutual exchange between humans who were open and curious about one another.

Then we made our way into Bolivia and things changed drastically yet again. We couldn't afford to take one of the nicer buses that were similar to a Greyhound bus in the US. Instead, we rode in an old school bus with no heat across the border from Argentina into Bolivia. The difference between the two countries was night and day. We went from a place with a mixed population of European and Indigenous people to nearly 100 percent Indigenous. In Bolivia, the soldiers were outwardly corrupt and even made a pass at me as I was crossing into their country. Here the border officers didn't take my passport, but they took a little bit of my dignity.

We were on an overnight bus headed to Potosí, which is a mining town with the biggest deposit of silver in the world. In fact, the Spanish founded Potosí as a mining town in 1545 and it was the location of the Spanish colonial silver mint for centuries.

It was also the city where one of my heroes lived. Her name was Domitila Barrios de Chungara. She was the wife of a miner, a feminist, and an Indigenous woman who had become a labor rights activist. Along with other miners' wives, she helped organize the Housewives' Committee to demand higher wages for miners. She became an international icon. I had read her autobiography *Si Me Permiten Hablar*, and she was my kind of feminist. I felt compelled to make a pilgrimage to where it had all started for her, deep in the silver mines of Potosí, where mining companies continued to extract the insides of Mother Earth for profit.

My brother and I were wearing T-shirts and shorts on the

bus. It had been hot and sunny when we'd boarded earlier that day. What we didn't realize, though, was that because of Bolivia's high elevation, the temperature drops dramatically once the sun sets. We woke up to thirty-degree weather and snow outside in the pitch black night. We were freezing and couldn't get to our bags to put on more clothing, so we had to hold on to each other for warmth.

We arrived at six in the morning and walked the desolate streets of Potosí with our backpacks. Once we got to our youth hostel, we quickly got into bed, but Jorge began to have a severe reaction to the altitude, telling me he couldn't breathe. Thoughts began racing through my head. *I'm only twenty years old. Can I even handle this? What am I supposed to do?*

I was terrified, so I went down to the lobby and told the hostel workers that my brother was having a hard time breathing. What could they do? I had read in our guidebook that there was a tea made with, believe it or not, the coca leaf, the same plant that cocaine comes from. Drinking the coca tea was supposed to help people slow down and breathe through the altitude sickness. They quickly brought tea to my brother and I stayed with him as he tried to calm down. Luckily, he didn't get any worse, and after a day or so of rest, we were able to explore.

I was fascinated by the people of Bolivia. The women wore bowler hats, beautiful petticoat skirts, and multicolored shawls. They often carried several children and the wares they sold along with them.

Most people in Bolivia didn't see us as adorable Mexicans, but as gringos, disliked by the Indigenous population because we looked like their oppressors. They had been treated inhumanely by their own people for too long. Despite making up the majority of the population, Indigenous people had no power there. The only thing they could do was look at us with disdain and hiss. They did not want to be gawked at by tourists. But I never gave up on trying to speak to everyone I met on the street. I told them that I was not a gringuita, I was Mexican.

When we got to the silver mines, we asked if we could go down and see them for ourselves. The local miners allowed Jorge and me to go down and make a quick trip in what appeared to be an elevator operated on a pulley inside a mountain. The passageways inside the mine were suffocating and claustrophobic. We came back up desperate for fresh air.

The song "Beast of Burden" by the Rolling Stones kept playing in my head as we walked through the streets of Potosí, and later La Paz and Cochabamba. The colonizers treated the Indigenous people here like beasts of burden, humans used to transport everything imaginable: sofas, beds, children, concrete, anything that could be carried on their backs.

Bolivia was the most politically unstable of the countries we had visited. If Brazil, Paraguay, and Argentina were all military dictatorships, then Bolivia was the land of the coup d'etats. "Coup d'etat" is a French term for what happens when an armed group, such as a militia, overthrows a ruling government by force, not through democratic processes like an election, and the new ruler seizes power. This is entirely different from a change of government brought on by the people through revolution, which changes or seeks to change the social system used to run the country with the intention of benefiting the people.

By the time we arrived in La Paz, the capital city, the country had already lived through more than one hundred eighty coups. On our third day in La Paz, the next coup d'etat occurred. The people at the youth hostel simply told us to stay inside for a couple days. The act of unseating people from office left and right had been normalized. Most of the coups were bloodless, but they were coups nonetheless.

Our last stop in Bolivia was Lake Titicaca on the border with Peru, the lake with the highest elevation in the world. I had always remembered the name Titicaca because it was funny sounding and I thought it was a place I would like to go one day. Our guidebook said there was a series of small islands in the middle of the lake called Taquile. The islands were run by women as part of a matriarchal government that was also socialist. Everything was equal. Everything was shared. It sounded a little bit like utopia.

Everybody who lived on the islands took responsibility for housing the few tourists they allowed to visit. We put our names down on a list and were granted permission to stay the night with one of the local families. A guide picked us up in a small boat and took us deep into the center of Lake Titicaca, which is one hundred eighteen miles long. After an hour and a half we arrived at our hosts' home. They lived in a small hut made of hardened mud held together by a wooden frame. It was one of three huts spaced out around an open fire pit. We would be sleeping in one of the other huts for the night. Inside there was a dirt floor and elevated beds made of wooden planks with a few animal hides thrown over them.

There was no electricity, no running water, nothing. It was as though life there had not changed from what it was like a hundred years before. The family fed us a simple, homemade meal and afterwards we sat around the fire and told funny stories. Their Spanish was very rudimentary because it was not their native language. It was a beautiful experience being able to spend time with people with whom I might have thought I had little in common. Everyone was in bed by nine o'clock. Without electricity, when the sun sets so do you, which is the opposite of twenty-four-hour New York City.

I was loving this communion with nature until around one in the morning, when I woke up because my stomach was rumbling. I had to use the bathroom. There were no toilets, of course, but I remembered that there was an area a short walk away where people could go do their business. I didn't know where I was and I didn't have a flashlight. I was dizzy and sick to my stomach. I knew I had to find my way there somehow, so I climbed off the bed and walked out into the pitch black night. I made my way to what I thought was the bathroom area and relieved myself. All I cared about was picking a spot far enough away from the house. I felt disgusting and humiliated and scared because there I was, half naked in what felt like the middle of nowhere.

But then, slowly, my eyes adjusted to the darkness. I looked up at the sky and it was on fire. There was no electric light anywhere around. For the first time in my life, I really saw the sky. The stars were so bright they were like street lights lighting the way for me back to the hut, bright enough to be lighting the streets of Park Avenue. I stood outside alone in the silence for one more moment before going back inside the dark hut. I wasn't afraid or disgusted any more. I was filled with awe.

There was a message in that sky for me: This is what your ancestors did. They looked at this sky and that was their everything. I was talking to the stars and they were talking to me. I was not in a rush. I was fine. I was in the middle of nowhere. I was okay.

The next day we were ferried out of Taquile and we moved on to Peru. Our first stop was Puno, a city that sits on the northwestern edge of Lake Titicaca. I made a trip to the open-air marketplace one day because I wanted to buy a sweater to stay warm in the winter weather. There was a woman selling blankets and sweaters and other things from one of the wooden stalls. She wore a bowler hat over long braids and her baby hung in a manta wrapped around her back.

Her name was Carlota and she told me her story. She was a single mom and belonged to a collective of Indigenous women artisans, just like my hero Domitila Chungara. She had joined because she believed in the power of the collective and said it was easier to run her business this way, even though she had to share a percentage of her profits and pay dues to the collective. They were safer because the police could not force them to move. As a result, she had a voice and she was working with other women, which made this market less cutthroat than the other ones in Puno.

I spent more than an hour talking to her while her baby

slept. It was the middle of the day in the middle of the week, so she could afford to take the time to speak to me. Carlota was surprised that I was so interested in her and that I wanted to know what she thought, how she lived her life, how she did things. I didn't realize it at the time, but I was thinking like a journalist. I was forming a bond with this stranger and giving her a chance to open up to me. I was reporting on the context of her life, which I could write about and share with others, giving her a voice in spaces that she couldn't reach on her own.

Carlota found me as curious as I found her. She asked me about living in New York City all by myself. What did my parents think? Did I have boyfriends? How did I handle that? I was twenty. She was around twenty-five. We talked about stuff that you usually don't talk about with somebody you just met. But to me, this was what feminism looked like—the ability to establish friendship, trust, and solidarity with other women. Finally, I said goodbye, loving this moment from my travels, knowing I would never forget this encounter.

But then at midnight that same night she showed up at my hostel with a friend and a bottle of pisco. They were both a little tipsy and each had their babies tied on their backs. Carlota told me that she wanted me to be the Madrina del Corte de Pelo or the godmother of her child's first haircut. So, at one in the morning, I cut her baby girl's hair.

Before they left, they asked me if they could ask me an intimate question. If I had boyfriends, how did I avoid getting pregnant? I told them about birth control and to always do what they needed to protect themselves.

Off they went, even more tipsy, walking through the deserted streets of Puno, Peru, their bowler hats tipping like they were, just off to the right. They giggled loudly without fear and walked like they owned the streets.

Jorge and I continued through Peru. We went to Machu Picchu, which was like a castle in the sky surrounded by lush clouds touching the mountain tops. We visited Ollantaytambo where the marketplace looked and smelled like a marketplace from hundreds of years ago. I was fascinated by these places that seemed untouched by time.

I bathed in the ancient hot springs of the Andes mountains that nature made for all of us, with men and women and kids in their underwear because they couldn't afford bathing suits. I drank in the pubs, not where the gringos went, but where the locals hung out. I was safe because I was with my brother.

By this point we had been traveling for six months. Originally, I had planned to return in the fall for the beginning of my junior year, but the months flew by and I was enjoying myself too much. So I decided to delay my return until the second semester of junior year, which began in January. But by December I had run out of money. I realized now that I was not going to make it back for second semester either.

After months of being tied at the hip, my brother and I split up. Because I had spent all my money on my travels, I had no choice but to fly back to Chicago, while Jorge, who still had money left, stayed in Mexico. My parents had agreed to cover my tuition, but I was responsible for my own living expenses. After all that time on the road, I was broke. I couldn't go back to Barnard and my beloved New York City until I saved up enough money again.

Instead of living in New York City after my glorious travels, I was back in Chicago waiting tables. Cecilia had taken over the radio show and life for her was continuing in the city. I was living back at home in my room, surrounded by the pink flowery wallpaper that I had come to resent. This was one of those moments when I couldn't see my own privilege. I had just witnessed people living in dire situations, fighting for their basic rights, fighting for jobs that paid them a living wage, fighting for just governments that didn't oppress their own people with violence. And here I was complaining about living in a bedroom with ugly wallpaper.

I was determined to go back to New York. I was working as many days a week as I could to put together the money to pay rent and finish school. After experiencing life so intensely, living in the moment, not having plans, I found myself in a completely different situation. I was yearning for my friends, my freedom back in New York, and a clear vision of what was going to happen next. But I didn't have it. Not yet.

CHAPTER 21

The Activist Becomes a Journalist

After waitressing for half a year while my classmates finished junior year, I had saved up enough money and returned to New York City in the fall to finish my studies at Barnard. Nini, Cecilia, and I reunited and I found us an apartment to live in together on 106th Street off Columbus Avenue. It was on the first floor in the back, with very little natural light, but it was what we could afford.

Nini had already graduated and got a job. Her father had made it safely out of Iran and her parents were now living in the Bronx. Cecilia's family continued to heal from the loss of her father, and she had a new boyfriend who sang Argentinian folk songs. We were three sisters from three different parts of the world, living our lives to the fullest, together on 106th Street. It was one of the happiest times in my life in New York. Though I was happy, I was also confused and often overwhelmed because everyone from my class had already graduated and moved on, and here I was back at my old haunts.

I was back on the air at WKCR with lots and lots of music and doing lots and lots of interviews with artists, musicians, and activists I had met through my travels in South America. It felt as if I was trying to catch up on all the hours of radio I had missed while I was gone. I took on a position of authority as one of the few women at the station and became the program manager of WKCR. Now the guys doing radio for Columbia University had to come to me for permission for various things.

There was a tremendous amount of mutual respect among all of us. My male colleagues saw me as a friend and partner, as someone they wanted to support. To this day, it remains one of the most collaborative places I've worked.

I was inspired by the multiday and week-long music festivals that the guys at WKCR who had been around for a long time would organize. For example, they had done a Bach festival that played classical music composed by Johann Sebastian Bach for four days straight, as well as marathons of Billie Holiday's love songs and music by John Coltrane to celebrate the jazz musician's birthday.

I decided that if they could do festivals, so could I. Following in the footsteps of the student activists who had founded the Latin music department, I felt it was about time that Columbia University's radio station hosted a Nueva Canción music festival in New York. So I stayed up for twenty-four hours and produced that event. Within a few months, I tried my hand at another major production by creating an eighteen-hour women's music and information festival for International Women's Day on March 8, 1982.

Then one of the guys at WKCR said, "Hey, Maria, I heard there's a music festival of Nueva Canción happening outside of Havana." The genre was being celebrated as a solid musical form that was deeply political. It was protest music inspired by Indigenous culture. It was the cry of the people with good beats. "Don't you think you should go?"

I looked at him and said, "Well, of course I do, but I'll never be able to get there."

He told me he would make it happen. It was incredibly forward-thinking of Columbia University to fund a student to document and record a Latin music festival in socialist Cuba, which had no political relations with the US at the time. I was going to a beautiful country that the US government had labeled an enemy. Off I went to Varadero, Cuba, for the Nueva Canción Festival. I recorded the whole thing on a reel-to-reel recorder that weighed a ton. Most of the time, I carried it by myself, but I was also good at asking for help.

By the time I returned, my music library was flourishing. In Cuba, I had gathered live music from the top Nueva Canción performers from across Latin America, which I played on WKCR. Now there was even a thriving Nueva Canción music scene in New York City. Musicians regularly performed at two speakeasies, one in Spanish Harlem, the other on the Lower East Side, to small audiences of thirty to fifty people. We were at the heart of it all. *Nueva Canción y Demás* had helped make it happen by exposing more people to this growing genre of Latin music.

The radio station halls were filled with the sounds of salsa, pan pipes, and claves and bongos. I had a life-changing moment at our funky old radio station studio when the musician Bobby Sanabria handed me a shaker while he and his band were doing a live set. He told me to feel the rhythm, and I realized I had the rhythm deep inside me.

Recognizing this, I became less self-conscious and let go of the need to be Latina enough for everyone else. I had proved I was Latina (to whom exactly? The Latino Identity Gods?). I had traveled through Latin America. I had perfected my Spanish. I had studied and read the great authors Gabriel Garcia Marquez, Juan Rulfo, Mario Vargas Llosa, Julio Cortazar, Jorge Luis Borges, Che Guevara, Sor Juana Inés de la Cruz, Gabriela Mistral, Elena Poniatowska, and so many others. I knew about politics from Brazil to Mexico.

I was, in fact, the Latin American New Yorker I had envisioned. Maybe it started when I saw the my first Frida Kahlo painting and I realized how free she was. Or maybe it was my feminist Mexican cousin who traveled on her own and inspired me to do the same. Or maybe it was hanging out late at night with the actors of *Zoot Suit*. I was forming this vision of myself. Independent. Radical. Feminista. I had become that woman and surrounded myself with other women, mostly Latinas and Afro-Latinas, who felt the same way about themselves. We celebrated one another by dancing to the rhythm of our lives, the ones we created for ourselves.

And as I finished up my senior year, I was spending all my time outside school at an epicenter of Latino and Latina dialogue and action. *Nueva Canción y Demás* had built up credibility with activists from around the country and Latin America. People trusted us. We were documenting a moment in history of Latino and Latina cultural resistance in New York City and beyond. We were activists building on the work of the Young Lords and the Black Panthers and giving voice to people making the same demands for justice and equity because of the deep poverty that still ravaged our communities in Harlem, Spanish Harlem, and the Bronx—neighborhoods that were just steps from our privileged existence at Barnard and the smelly college radio studio at Columbia. And not just in those communities of New York City, but all throughout Latin America.

The war in El Salvador was intensifying and the United States had made it clear what side they were on. Instead of supporting the people who wanted change and justice, they began sending a million dollars a day to the El Salvador military, an institution that had committed documented human rights abuses. We began to play music and updates from the rebel radio stations and guerrilla strongholds in the mountains of El Salvador on the airwaves of New York City—to anyone listening on Broadway and in El Barrio, Washington Heights, Queens, and the South Bronx Boogie Down.

There was a genocide going on in Guatemala. A general named Efraín Ríos Montt, who was a Christian evangelical, had taken over the country and was killing tens of thousands of Indigenous people through government-sanctioned massacres. Rigoberta Menchú, a feminist and human rights activist, survived one of these massacres and lived to tell the story. She later received the Nobel Peace Prize for her courageous work and accepted the award in full Indigenous dress and spoke in her Mayan language, K'iche'. Even she found a way and came to speak to us in the studio on *Nueva Canción y Demás* one night.

The Sandinista Revolution in Nicaragua, a movement powered by the people to take down an unjust dictator, was also under attack by President Ronald Reagan's administration. The United States didn't like the Sandinista government because it was too progressive for US interests, so the US started an undercover war (most people didn't know it was even going on) by supplying money to the forces who were against the Sandinistas, the counter-revolutionaries, or Contras. As part of this secret war, the US government attempted to secretly sell illegal arms to Iran and then use the profits to fund the Contras in Nicaragua to take down the people's revolution there. When this corrupt scheme came to light, it was known as the Iran-Contra affair, and it's just one example of how the US has been wreaking havoc in Central America for decades—only to act all surprised when the people they're destabilizing end up coming to seek refuge in the north from all the violence.

The poetry of my happy and fulfilled life was coming into direct contact with people who had survived war and political unrest in Latin America. People were forced to leave their countries simply because they wanted justice. Activists from Central America, especially El Salvador, Nicaragua, and Guatemala, would stop by our radio show every week. I met Salvadoran refugees who had escaped to New York City, whose families had been targeted, whose villages had been bombed. I asked guests on the show to tell us their stories. Often it was hard to hear all the suffering they had been through, but it was the truth.

Earlier refugees from Chile and Argentina were now meeting the latest refugees from El Salvador and Guatemala who had made it to the safety of the Upper West Side. Everybody was working together in coalition. The radio show became an underground community of activists, musicians, artists, and revolutionaries. No one in the mainstream knew about us or understood what we were doing, but the people who mattered knew what we stood for and that gave us street cred. How do you get that kind of respect? You have to earn it by working at something honestly and authentically.

Everything I had learned and experienced during college was coming to a head and I felt I had to make a decision: Was I going to be an artist or was I going to be an activist? Could I do both of these non-professions and survive? The arts in New York were highly competitive. Whether it was theater or dance, I always felt like I wasn't good enough. The city was full of professional artists and actors and dancers who were dedicating their lives to their art. Was training to become a dancer and performer going to be the best way for me to contribute to the fight for justice in Central America? Should I become an organizer or a full-time activist like some of the people I had met? Or should I dig deeper into the persona I had developed as a radio journalist, documenter of reality, interviewer, community builder?

I decided I was going to be an activist. I hung out with activists all the time now because they would come to the radio show and we'd go out afterward. I was learning about humanity up close and personal, not just reading about it in my Latin American history class.

All of this came together in a moment of combustion. The situation for Salvadoran refugees in the United States had become dire. The US government was deporting them and sending them back to the war-torn towns and frontline battles they had narrowly escaped. Young Salvadoran refugees decided to make a statement and put their lives on the line by staging a hunger strike on the steps of Riverside Church in Manhattan. This wasn't something that was happening far away, like Cesar Chavez and Dolores Huerta's grape boycott in California. These were people my age, some of whom were my friends, using political protest to demand legal status for themselves and their fellow refugees right in my neighborhood.

The hunger strike got a lot of attention from the news media and soon there were reporters from national publications like *The New York Times* and international newspapers as far away as Japan that wanted to interview the hunger strikers. Since I spoke both English and Spanish fluently, I helped journalists connect with the people involved in the movement and translated for them. I filled them in on the cultural and political context of what was going on and these professional reporters treated me with respect. Of course, none of them were Latinas and there were very few women, but I was getting a taste of how reporters in the

United States worked. *Hmm*, I thought, *I bet I could do this*.

The hunger strike wasn't just a news story for me, though. I was worried for my Salvadoran friends who were abstaining from eating in protest. Each day they got weaker. Meanwhile, my friends David, Chris, Tammis, and Cecilia were angry that New Yorkers weren't paying attention to the war in El Salvador even though their tax dollars were being used to fund it. Together we designed an impromptu group action in front of Radio City Music Hall, the famous concert venue at Rockefeller Center.

Whenever the lights turned red in the intersection outside Radio City on Sixth Avenue, we would rush into the street and lie down as if we had been massacred—it was what's called a "die-in." Instead of a sit-in protest where you sit down in a public space and refuse to leave, we dropped on the ground like dead bodies to visually represent the violence going on in Central America.

I also joined the Asociación de Mujeres de El Salvador and attended meetings once or twice a week. We organized cultural events, dance recitals with progressive artists, and poetry readings with poets like Adrienne Rich, Carolyn Forché, and June Jordan to raise awareness about the war going on there and raise money for Salvadoran women and children refugees. Most of these artists had never been to El Salvador, but they contributed to the cause because of a beautiful word: solidarity.

I was leading protest rallies because I had a green card and was not in danger of being deported. I understood when the Salvadoran refugee women around me said, "Speak for us, please. We can't do it ourselves. We don't speak English and some of us are not supposed to be here in this country. Will you do this for us?" How could I say no? I led a rally in the middle of Times Square. I spoke on behalf of my friends, not as a Salvadoran, but as a Mexican immigrant, and told their stories of being gunned down in the streets of San Salvador just for protesting.

I was beginning to understand that being a person who lived in multiple realities was a superpower. I was the program director of WKCR. I was an activist on the street. I was a disc jockey. I was a journalist. I was a student studying feminism.

I continued to be a border crosser, only this time I was bringing more people with me. People who didn't speak Spanish were now listening to the radio show and starting to take Spanish classes. I helped translate for the Spanish-speaking people on the front lines so that their words could reach English-speaking journalists and get printed on the front page of *The New York Times*.

I was no longer living in the moment, as I had when I was a carefree traveler, because the stories that made up my world now were filled with such sadness. The importance of the experiences I'd had in the streets of Lima, La Paz, Asunción, Potosí, Rio de Janeiro, and Mexico City were becoming clearer to me. Throughout it all, I had been fascinated and inspired by the strength of Latin American women and how they formed collective organizations to support one another and fight for justice.

I declared my major in women's studies. To graduate and

complete my degree, I was required to write a thesis paper. At first, I thought my thesis could focus on the women I had met on my travels, like the miners' wives in Potosí and Carlota in Puno, the women protesting for democracy on the streets of La Paz, the indigenous women running everything on the island of Taquile. It had taken me almost a year to save up the money to be able to do that trip and it seemed impossible that I'd be able to go back and find the same people again. I had to figure out how to write a thesis without needing to travel and raise the money to do so.

The answer was staring me in the face: I would write my thesis about the Salvadoran women refugees who were right in front of me, whose stories I had become so familiar with, and whose lives as refugees in the US I had witnessed up close. I decided to interview Salvadoran women who were living on Long Island to avoid writing about the people who were already a part of my life. I had enough academic ethics and understanding to know that if I was going to do empirical research like this, I had to be somewhat removed from my subjects.

There were a lot of Salvadorans arriving in Long Island, in Hempstead and Westbury, at the time. I made contact with a church that was providing frontline services for recently arrived Salvadoran women refugees. I traveled out there on many occasions and interviewed women, most of whom were in their twenties. A few were in their thirties. Many of them had not talked about these traumatic experiences before, unless they had applied for asylum. Many of them were undocumented, so I had to be careful about how much I asked them to reveal about themselves.

The most challenging aspect of this project was the fact that I was interviewing people who were close to my own age. They had previously lived normal lives. Maybe they were poor, but for the most part their lives were not under threat. Then suddenly because of the war they had been forced to leave their homes.

One of the young women I interviewed was particularly sad and sullen. She was seventeen years old and I had a hard time connecting with her. She was not very expressive and I thought that maybe I had done something wrong. As I was getting ready to leave after an interview with another woman, I saw the seventeen-year-old outside playing basketball some-what strenuously with a group of younger kids. The social worker who had connected me with these women said, "It's really sad, what's happening."

"Why?" I asked, confused. "They're playing basketball. Is something wrong?"

"She's playing with that ball because she wants to lose the pregnancy," the social worker said.

She was pregnant and she didn't want to be. *Oh my God, it can't be that*, I thought. *This young woman is reduced to having to play basketball and hoping that she gets injured and somehow loses the pregnancy. How can I live in the same world where something like that is happening? How can I be a feminist in this world?*

After conducting dozens of interviews, I compiled all the women's stories and wrote about the greater historical context of the war in El Salvador. I submitted my thesis and it was read by Peter Juviler, one of the most esteemed professors of political science at Barnard. He gave me an A.

In doing the research for and writing my thesis, I got the sense that I was on the path to something I wanted to spend the rest of my life doing.

I was becoming a budding journalist. Although I never would have spoken those words aloud, I was letting myself make connections and follow my intuition. My skills as a reporter were confirmed by the work I did at the radio station and the multiple interviews I conducted every week. But the imposter monster still made me doubt myself.

My eyes were open to the world around me now and that wasn't going to change. I had learned about the situation in El Salvador from the community I was a part of as a Latina, an activist, and a DJ. I realized I was in a position to help tell that story in the United States in a way that no one else was telling it.

When I was a girl, stories of war had always felt like something that happened far away. Yet the war was actually always within my reach. Just like the stories that are happening around you today. They're within your reach if you open your eyes and look for them.

CHAPTER 22

Learning How to Say My Name

Reality began to hit me as I started my last semester at Barnard in the fall of 1984. All my friends had graduated and were long gone. Now that the end of college was in sight, I realized I hadn't done a single internship and had nothing to put on my resume. The truth was that I couldn't afford to do unpaid internships because I was always waiting tables to pay for my living expenses and rent.

Mom and Dad never put pressure on me to get good grades or to apply to specific schools, because they knew I worked hard. It helped that I was the youngest of four children, and my parents were each busy with their own work. Dad was working closely with the team that would soon invent the cochlear implant and give hearing to the deaf, and Mom had become a full-fledged activist defending the rights of women and survivors of domestic violence at Mujeres Latinas En Accion. But now that I was about to graduate, they were starting to ask, "What are you going to do?"

Like any college student who is about to get tossed into the real world, I was nervous and a little scared. I didn't want to face having to choose a career and a job. Maybe I could just be a waitress forever. It meant I had cash in hand all the time. What was so bad about that?

My friends had each wandered off the beaten path and were piecing together a different kind of lifestyle than the ones you might expect of Barnard and Columbia grads. David was driving a cab. Tammis was a bike messenger in Los Angeles, where she was trying to break in as a film editor. Cecilia was living in Peru and contemplating a master's degree. I was finishing college while waiting tables and working at WKCR.

Still, the pressure of graduating from an Ivy League institution was real. I was surrounded by classmates who were making plans for their futures and talking about big jobs with big salaries. I didn't want to be a part of that. Yes, I wanted a job, but I wanted a job that meant something to me. Being on the right side of justice, calling out war mongers and dictators and the silencing of innocent people, standing up for the rights of immigrants and refugees, defining myself and finding myself—these things were more important to me than making a lot of money.

For the first time, I forced myself to go to the career center on campus. My hands were trembling as I leafed through the huge internship binder with listings for ABC News, *The New York Times*, and *New York* magazine. All I kept saying was *nope, nope, nope*. Then I stopped on the clear plastic folder from

National Public Radio (NPR). It was an internship named for Susan Stamberg (a Barnard alumna, and now I began to understand the perks of privilege) who was the anchor for the network's most important show, *All Things Considered*. The internship was based in Washington, D.C., but another Barnard alumna would provide free housing (more perks!). But my imposter syndrome monster took over. *Nope, I could never get that*, I said to myself, and leafed past it.

After half an hour, I found two internships that I was excited about and thought I might have a shot at—the international Lawyers' Committee for Human Rights and the Institute for Policy Studies, which was a progressive think tank. I thought I could be an academic or maybe a lawyer who does international policy work. Both were in D.C. but did not come with housing.

I was sitting at the table, probably looking a little overwhelmed, when a woman who worked in the office came and sat with me. Jane was calm and patient and asked me what I had done during my time at Barnard. I talked to her about my thesis and work documenting the hunger strike. I told her about WKCR and the twenty-four-hour music festivals I had produced. I told her about the authors and musicians and other journalists I had interviewed. She listened intently and with such curiosity.

"You're missing one application," she pointed out.

"What's that?" I asked.

"You must apply to NPR. You must."

"Really, do you think so?" I said. "I'm not good enough."

There was no way I could imagine getting an internship at NPR, even though so many experiences from my life were pointing me in that direction.

"Oh, yes you are," Jane insisted, "You are good enough. You're wonderful. Apply." Her conviction in me validated my years on air anchoring for WKCR and reminded me that even though I'd gotten a B in the only journalism class I ever took, I already had several bylines in the college newspaper.

I applied to the internship at NPR and left WKCR's phone number as my contact. At that point, I spent almost all my free time at the radio station, since I had continued on as program director and had a lot of responsibilities.

One day while I was working, Phil Schaap, a jazz DJ who was about to go on the air, came into the studio where I was logging tapes and told me there was someone on the phone for me. I thought it was a regular business call or a listener complaint. Instead, it was Ted Clark at NPR, the mild-mannered executive producer of *All Things Considered*, calling to offer me the internship. When I imagined big media networks like NPR, I assumed the people who worked there were superhuman. But on the other end of the line was a normal sounding, middle-aged man. He wasn't anything like the brassy male journalists I was used to watching on television, and I connected with that.

After I hung up and the news finally sunk in, I started screaming and jumping for joy because I was in a soundproof studio. Schaap—we called each other by our last names—was on the air in the other studio but he started applauding from behind the glass. He could see how life-changing this would be.

The internship was at NPR's headquarters in Washington, D.C., and was set to begin in January 1985. It came with a commuter stipend and free housing—a private room in a Barnard alumna's home. Normally, the internship only lasted two weeks, but since I would be finished with school after December, I volunteered to stay for a full month.

As I was finishing up my coursework and finalizing my thesis those last few weeks of 1984, I took on as many waitressing shifts as I could handle. I wanted to save enough money to cover my expenses for the month I'd be living in D.C. My friends in the restaurant business, all actors and writers, were some of my biggest fans. They had encouraged me to apply for the internship, supported me as I prepared to move to Washington, and gave me some of their extra shifts so I could make more money by working doubles.

My friends from the movement cheered me on, too. One of their own was now going to be a part of mainstream American journalism. My mom and dad respected NPR and listened to it occasionally, more so now because of this. They were super proud of me and saw that my life was beginning to take shape.

My nerves were met with excitement, but also deep feelings of inadequacy. To prepare, I started listening to NPR's *Morning Edition* and *All Things Considered* religiously on my portable AM/FM Walkman radio as I walked to and from my final classes across campus.

On the first Sunday of January, I woke up early and jumped on the subway to Penn Station. From there I boarded an eight a.m. Amtrak train to Washington, D.C. Since my gig started on Monday, I had decided to get there a day early so I could get situated and oriented in this new city. I arrived at the old D.C. train station four hours later and made my way with my luggage to the Metro. It was so quiet and clean compared to New York City, except the train cars were carpeted, which I thought was gross and weird. New Yorkers would not be down with that!

My host didn't actually live in D.C., but in Arlington, Virginia, just across the state line. When I stepped out of the Metro station in Arlington, there was no one on the streets. It was like one of those horror films where you wake up and everybody has disappeared. The city was all tall, sleek, shiny buildings in empty downtown streets with no numbers and no street signs. I still had to walk the distance between the Metro and my host's home. This was before the era of Google Maps, and since there was no one on the street, I couldn't ask anyone for help. I just started walking, lugging my suitcase behind me, until I found a store that was open. I went in and they sent me more or less in the right direction.

The address was for a twelve-story luxury apartment complex at the top of the hill. By the time I made it up to the entrance, the wheels on the suitcase were falling off. It appeared no one had ever walked there from the Metro because everyone had cars. When the doorman saw me huffing up the driveway, he ran down to meet me.

"Barbara Colby," I said to him, a bit exasperated, repeating the name of my host, who had graduated from Barnard in

1942. I could tell just from the lobby that this was the fanciest building I had ever lived in. There were lots of mirrors and gold trim. The doorman took me up to Mrs. Colby's apartment, which was a two-story duplex with floor-to-ceiling glass windows and an outdoor terrace with a view of Washington, D.C., in the distance. It reeked of wealth and I was weirded out by it, but I was also really curious and intrigued. I started to imagine that these scenes from my life were all part of a movie and that I simply needed to watch and smile.

Mrs. Colby was a sweet older woman with dyed-blond hair curled in the style of Betty White. I wondered how I would build a friendship with Mrs. Colby, which is how she liked to be addressed.

After I dropped my bag off in the guest room, I excused myself so I could get back on the Metro and figure out my commute for the next day. I had to be at NPR at nine a.m. and I was not going to be late or lost. Creating a plan of action and trying to minimize all the things that could go wrong was one way I could combat my nerves.

Once I got back, I stepped into my host's expansive living room. The full moon was rising over the Potomac River and the Capitol Building was lit up, shining like a white sun in the pitch-black night, the lights of the Lincoln Memorial slicing the darkness with a beam pointed skyward. It was breathtaking. Suddenly, I was filled with gratitude. My life *was* a movie.

I turned around and joined Mrs. Colby in the kitchen, where she was making a simple oven-baked chicken breast, iceberg lettuce salad with a packaged Italian dressing, and instant "minute rice" that I had only ever seen in TV commercials. Mrs. Colby poured herself a glass of white wine, or maybe it was her second by now, and asked me to join her. The *PBS News Hour* was on in the background and Mrs. Colby began to talk about the people on the TV as if she knew them—the vice president, a cabinet member, the anchor of the show. It slowly dawned on me that proper Mrs. Colby was no shrinking violet in this town.

It turned out her ex-husband was William E. Colby, the former director of the CIA. I tried to hide my shock as I listened to her criticize the famous politicians and members of President Ronald Reagan's cabinet that she knew personally. It was an important reminder that the men in power were flawed human beings just like the rest of us. Mrs. Colby made me see how distant I was from the circles that wield power and influence in the United States. Yet at the same time, living in Barbara Colby's house and working at NPR meant I was one step closer.

The two sides of my life were once again colliding in a way that I never could have predicted.

The journalist and activist in me realized I had information about individuals who were involved in helping to overthrow an abusive government in El Salvador. I was now sleeping in the house of the former director and "spymaster" of the CIA, a government institution that had been meddling in Latin American affairs for decades. Did CIA agents search Mrs. Colby's home after she had strange visitors? Would they suspect me of being a spy because I had relationships with Central American activists? Was I endangering anyone I knew by being here?

If I was going to be a journalist, it was becoming clear I could no longer be an activist. Trying to do both would compromise my integrity in both pursuits and possibly endanger my activist friends, and on my end, my career. Similarly, news publications would assume I could not be objective or impartial if I was already loyal to a specific movement. A feeling of melancholy fell over me because I knew that my life as an activist would have to come to an end if I truly wanted to pursue a career as a journalist.

On my first day at NPR, I half-expected the office to be a bigger version of WKCR, but I was wrong. It felt huge but cramped, too. There were lots of cubicles crammed up against one another, newspapers scattered on tables, and typewriters on every desk. When I walked into the newsroom, everyone looked much more grown-up and serious than I had imagined. In the middle of the room there was a whiteboard divided up into thirds, with each section representing thirty minutes of airtime on *All Things Considered*, creating a visual schedule for how the show would run. Each line listed the title of the piece, the last name of the reporter, and the length of the story.

Most of the employees were men, which was not unusual given my experience at WKCR, and most were white. There were a few young women on staff, only one of whom was Black. By now I was used to feeling like a fish out of water, like a phony, because I had been feeling that way since my first day of high school. Here it was again, my old friend the imposter syndrome monster.

I didn't say much that first day. Everyone was pleased to

meet me. Susan Stamberg, after whom the internship was named because she was a Barnard graduate, gave me a big hug and was the sweetest person of all. But she was the anchor of *All Things Considered* and the star of the network, so her busy schedule didn't give her much free time to spend with me.

I was assigned to follow Ellen Weiss, who was then the best production assistant on the show, known for her speed. She could cut a fifteen-minute interview down to four minutes in less than thirty minutes. I liked her and could see parts of myself in her—kind of like that moment in Pilsen when Beatriz showed me another version of myself, except Ellen was Jewish and white. But I could see that Ellen was strong and determined. She walked around in tight pants and brown-and-white cowboy boots, the kind you can afford to buy when you have a job. I wanted a real job like that.

After a week or two of following several producers around, I got the hang of how things worked there. Producers pitched story ideas in the morning meetings. If their story was given the okay, they made phone calls to set up an interview. The anchor would do the interview. The producer would listen in and take notes, go into the studio, and in rapid speed, take razorblades and cut the audio tape of the interview down by hand. They would write an introduction and get it done before *All Things Considered* went on the air later that same day.

My time was running out. I was already halfway through my month-long internship and no one had shown much interest in me or asked me to contribute any ideas. I was disappearing into the background. I could not let that happen.

The Mexican immigrant in me decided that *would not* happen. I geared myself up to try and make a one-minute spot for the news headlines at the top of the show. It was a ridiculous dream to think I could end up on the air, but then again, people thought my dad's dream was ridiculous when he was back in Mexico, too.

Ronald Reagan was about to be sworn in as president for his second term and *All Things Considered* was planning their coverage of the official event. I, however, knew about the unofficial protests that were being organized. I was sitting on a story that no one else had brought up.

I looked for someone I thought could be an ally. The newscasts were produced in a separate part of the newsroom, where they were anchored by Lori Waffenschmidt in the evenings and Carl Kassel during the day. Lori seemed like a sweet, normal human being and less high-strung than the women on *All Things Considered,* who wanted more power but were working for men. Lori was a woman with power. She was the one who decided what would end up in her newscast, so I decided that I needed to find the guts to ask another woman for guidance, as I had learned from studying at a women's college. That was the least I could do for myself.

I was shaking when I approached Lori but I forced myself to speak. I told her about the anti-Reagan protest and asked if she would like me to report on it for their Reagan inauguration coverage. The organizers wanted to draw attention to the bombings in El Salvador under Reagan by protesting the celebration of his second term. Without thinking twice, she said yes. And unlike most of the other producers, she spent time talking to me, telling me what to do, what to get in the field, how to sign out the equipment, and where I could sit and use a typewriter.

I went home to Mrs. Colby's luxurious duplex and told her I had my first official assignment. The wife of the former head of the CIA thought covering the protests against Reagan's inauguration was a great way to start my career at NPR. Mrs. Colby was more progressive than I could have ever imagined, which taught me another lesson about trying not to be so judgmental.

The next day I signed out one of the big clunky cassette recorders that NPR had stacked in a closet and learned how to operate it. I had to make sure to hit the record and play buttons at the same time, otherwise nothing would get recorded on the tape. I also had to wear bulky headphones so that I could listen to the playback as people spoke into my microphone. NPR gave me a pen, a reporter's notebook, and a press pass so that people would know I was a working journalist.

For the first time, I attended a protest not as an activist or a participant, but as a journalist representing a national news network. I did my best to ask difficult questions of supporters on both sides of the issue. That meant I had to stop people in the middle of the protest and ask them to speak to me while other protestors were screaming and chanting all around us. I was nervous and shaking all over as I held the microphone to people's faces for their comments. I kept obsessing over the fact that I was certainly missing something.

I took the Metro back to NPR headquarters, listened to the tape, logged it, and cut it down to two short interviews with some street sounds from the protest. I typed up a script and handed it over to Lori, who treated me like a peer, not an intern. She read it and made a few corrections here or there, tightening up a sentence or two and making sure I referred to Reagan as President Reagan. Then she told me to record it, and I did. I signed off at the end of the piece by saying my name with an English pronunciation.

My first piece for NPR was going to be on the air that night and I had no way to tell anybody. We didn't have cell phones back then and making long distance calls was extremely expensive. Lori let me use one of NPR's phones to call my parents. The only person I could get through to was the secretary at my dad's laboratory, and she put him on.

"Papi, I'm going to be on the radio tonight!" I squealed.

Papi was a little confused at first, but he congratulated me and told me how proud he was. I found an empty editing room and sat down by myself to listen to the show live, which was pumped in through the speakers in all the editing booths.

When I heard my spot on the air, I cried, all alone in that tiny booth. All of the hard work and all of those long nights on the radio at WKCR, just learning how to find my voice, had paid off. I knew I had the privilege of being in these places with powerful people, but I was defining myself on my own terms. It all felt very risky because it was. But in the short term, I had proven to myself that I could do it. I felt like I had earned my spot at NPR. The tears made me feel like a little girl but I was smiling like a young woman, too.

Lori told me I did a great job, and then I told her about

another protest. This time, conservative activists were demonstrating against immigration reform at the headquarters of the Immigration and Naturalization Service. Reagan was disliked by the Latino left but he was also disliked by the conservative anti-immigrant academics and think tanks who taunted him for granting "amnesty" to undocumented people.

Lori was thrilled to have fresh material for her newscast. The day I went into the studio to record my second news spot, I realized I had a big decision to make: Who was I going to be? Was I going to say my name in English or Spanish?

So much of my life in New York was lived in Spanish. I studied and read in Spanish. My friends from El Salvador all spoke Spanish. Our meetings and my own WKCR radio show were in Spanish. I was back to speaking Spanish with Mom and Dad as I reclaimed my mother tongue.

I knew whatever way I chose to say my name was going to stick with me forever. I also knew I had to be me. I was either going to fade into the background from trying too hard to fit in or I was going to shine by being my authentic self.

I sat alone in the edit booth and read the spot aloud over and over again, pronouncing my name in English and then in Spanish.

It felt natural to say my name in English because I'd been doing it my whole life. No one ever said to me, "What a beautiful name! Why didn't you say it in Spanish?" Si, I Americanized it because I had no other model to show me how to challenge that convention.

I thought, *It's easy to say your name in English. Easier for everyone. You won't hear complaints from anyone.* But I had never gone for easy. My otherness had always pushed me to take those risks because I was already seen as an outsider. What did I have to lose?

I said my name in Spanish aloud and it sounded like such a revolutionary thing to do. It was subtle and yet, totally in your face. I was speaking perfect Ivy league-educated English and then BOOM . . . my name in perfect Spanish!

And just like that, I decided to make listeners do a double take.

No one had done that on national radio or TV before.

I thought about the listeners, most of them white Americans, tuned in to public radio. Saying my name the way it was meant to be said was my way of telling them, *You may think I am so different from you, but really, I am you.*

In the last two weeks of my internship I'd been able to get on the air twice. People heard that the quiet intern from Barnard had ended up voicing a spot for the newscast and had sounded as good as any other reporter on the air. I was beginning to believe in myself.

I had grown up with so much self-doubt, yet I had made this happen. It was real even though I felt like I was in a dream. I stood up in the edit room, turned off the light, and let the tingles run through my body. The butterflies weren't in my stomach. They were in my chest. I had to hold myself, wrap my arms around myself.

The choices you make when you're just starting out in the world, like when you are alone in an editing booth the size of a small closet, can be incredibly exhilarating. I was betting on myself, jumping off the deep end, getting comfortable with the butterflies, pushing myself on stage—only this time the stage was a national news organization and it turned out the whole country would be listening.

I had to take myself seriously. I had to eat my fear and become the journalist my country needed me to be. Committed. Questioning. Unafraid (well, maybe a little afraid, but still unstoppable). Mexican. Immigrant. American. Woman. Me.

And when I did—ten cuidado because nothing could stop me.

Epilogue

That imposter monster has followed me throughout my career as a journalist. But I pushed it down and never let that little voice scare me enough to stop me from doing what I needed to do.

It was the immigrant voice in the back of my head telling me to take up space that made me do it.

Do what, you may ask?

That risky move, to say my name in Spanish, to stand out and be able to stand up for why, ended up bringing attention to me in a positive way. I went on to be the first Latina journalist in almost all the newsrooms that I worked in. My first full-time job in journalism was as a production assistant at NPR. I worked at CBS News and did local public radio at WNYC. My dream job was to be the first Latina correspondent at NPR. Once I knew that was the gig I wanted, I said it out loud. Five years later I made it happen.

My first year as a journalist, I realized that even though I wasn't wealthy or white, I did have privilege. If I was the first Latina to be there, in any space, then I had a responsibility to show up for my comunidad, which is largely people of color and underrepresented communities. I had to push through feeling scared or uncomfortable because I owed it to them to bring their stories into the all-white newsrooms run by men that I had gained entrance to.

In 1985, I was hired at NPR as a special reporter covering Latino issues, in part because of political pressure from media activists like Maria Emilia Martin. She was the founding executive producer of a show called *Latino USA*, and she changed my life when she asked me to anchor it. Today I am the executive producer and anchor of *Latino USA*. When the show first started, critics (and they are everywhere) said it would last maybe three to five years. In 2023, we will celebrate thirty years on the air.

Guess who is getting the last risa, the last laugh?

From NPR, I went on to be hired as the first Latina correspondent at CNN and then at PBS. Along the way, I got married to an incredible Afro-Taino artist and had two kids. It wasn't all rosy. Behind the scenes, my ego got so big to survive the battles in the media that it almost cost me my family. It is hard to be a journalist who is also a woman of color, a Latina, and an immigrant, but I shouldn't have brought those battles into my home. With time, I had to learn how to stop trying to be the producer with my own family. As my daughter once said, "I don't want Maria Hinojosa here. I want my mom."

Remember that Mexican saying, no hay mal que por bien no venga? There is no bad from which good cannot come. In 2010 I had been a journalist for more than twenty years and suddenly it looked like I was going to be out of a job. Desperate and feeling like I had nothing to lose, I got in touch with *60 Minutes*. They agreed to speak to me! I was so excited, until the executive asked me over coffee if I could wait until one of the older white men on their staff got sick or died before they offered me a job. Was this a joke, an insult, or real? After that meeting, I got on the subway and cried on the A train all the way home to 125th Street in the heart of Harlem.

That's when I decided to create my own company. I had never done anything like that before, but I found people who believed in my mission of using journalism to tell the true narrative of Latinos and Latinas, people of color, immigrants, and other often-overlooked communities, and invited them to join me.

I founded Futuro Media in 2010 as a nonprofit media company. Many people saw it as a risky move and gave it three to five years at most. Futuro is reflective of the newsroom I have always wanted to work in, where our voices, not those of straight white men, are centered and nobody has to feel imposter syndrome. As I write this, Futuro Media is turning eleven years old.

I take great inspiration from Frederick Douglass, a man who was born into slavery but then became a free man. He not only wrote about his own experiences, but also founded *The North Star*, the first Black newspaper in the country. I aspire to continue the legacy of Jovita Idar and Ida B. Wells and Ed Bradley and Ruben Salazar, all influential journalists in turbulent times. This thought is both humbling and empowering.

Many times I have found myself overwhelmed by the job in front of me. Frankly, I'm scared a lot of the time. It's not like I have a playbook for how to do this. In these moments, I find myself walking to the statue of Frederick Douglass a few blocks from my home. I think about what he had to face as a journalist and abolitionist in the US. Or I walk to the statue of Harriet Tubman that's around the corner and I think about what she did, walking ninety miles or more each time she brought a group of Black people to freedom in the North via the Underground Railroad.

I am sure they were both terrified many times in their lives as Americans of conscience.

This calms my heart. They paved the way for how progress can be fought for and won in this country if you believe in full-bodied democracy. If you want change, you have to make it yourself and build the plane as you are flying it.

I keep on dreaming and creating because that is who we are as people who love this country.

Decades after I arrived in the U.S., when my mom told me that the immigration agents had almost taken me away from her, I understood a deeper reason why I had always felt so passionately about the issue of immigration. Not all immigrants who are reporters cover immigration or even care about it, but for me it was a keystone. My first story for NPR was about an immigration protest. Immigration has been at the heart of so much of my work for decades, so many people's stories I've had the privilege of sharing with the world.

Trauma can live in our bones. And like those little seeds that are planted in your life, trauma plants its own seeds. But not all those seeds grow into pain. Some can flower into our deepest purpose.

I hope this book helps you to ask the questions you need answered in your life. That may take some time, but when you find you have questions about the world around you, start jotting them down. Do you know the story of how you came to live in this country? Did you see parts of your own story in mine? Did it make you more curious about who you are? I hope so. What will you do to help make this country the place we want it to be? It's your turn now to find your voice and your power. You are not invisible to me.

I see you because once I was you.

ACKNOWLEDGMENTS

A book is written by an author, but there is almost always a team involved in getting the book ready for publication, so you never feel that alone. My team is led by my wonderful agent Adriana Dominguez who planted the seed to write this book for younger readers. That seed was watered by my personal editor Katie Gee Salisbury who encouraged me to do this work because, truthfully, I was scared.

Our little seed found a home and flourished under the gentle guidance of the editor of the Young Readers Edition of *Once I Was You*, Kendra Levin. You wouldn't be holding this book in your hands if it wasn't for Kendra. Thank you!

I lost two primos to COVID during the year I wrote this book, and so Gernardo Peña and Enrique Gomez will always be tied to this book.

I want to say a special thank you to my family and colegas who have been a part of the *Once I Was You* family. Lili Ruiz es mi inspiración y mano derecha and an *OIWY* pillar. Maria Yurema Guadalupe de los Indios Perez Hinojosa es mi hija querida, my joy, and also a key part of Team *OIWY*. Gracias mijita! Raul Ariel Jesús De Todos Santos Perez Hinojosa es mi hijo and mi otra mano derecha and the one who keeps me calm and tells me to breathe. Gracias for all you do.

Thank you to our cover artist, Paola Escobar, and to Luna Arce-Rueda who offered insightful feedback on an early draft of this book.

Much gratitude for everyone who is a part of Futuro Media and who gave me the time and space to write. Thank you to Peter Platt and my Barnard College English Department colleagues for their support and to my students who always listen and egg me on with love and anticipation.

Para mi familia en este lado, en el otro lado y en todos los lados, gracias por el amor. Entre nosotros no puede haber fronteras. Love must transcend the walls other humans build to separate us.

Finally, to my husband, Gérman Perez, and Walter, Safiya, Miko, and Benito, who, year after year, are there for me.